Psychology · Slander · Intuition

PSI

*P*sychology
*S*lander
*I*ntuition

Dr Paul Brown
in association with
Steve Knight, Mike Whitehill
and Danny Kishon

PICTORIAL
PRESENTATIONS
SOUVENIR PRESS

CONTENTS

A NOTE OF THANKS

To Dr James Thompson and Margaret Ballard who helped set us on our way. To Jacqui who helped mould the final result, also Angela and Sharon.

And in particular Cath and Pip who put up with the writing of the book.

A GUIDE TO PSI

Welcome to the world of Psychology, Slander and Intuition. PSI for short.

Apart from this book, the concept of PSI has set in motion a novel form of assessing people's perceptions of themselves and others, a best-selling board game, and a forthcoming TV Game Show.

The book itself follows an interdisciplinary approach where the Psychology is provided courtesy of Paul Brown (PhD.Dip Psych.FBPsS.), and the Slander and Intuition are supplied from the experiences of Steve Knight, Mike Whitehill and Danny Kishon.

We have tried to make this book accessible to skimmers as well as readers. If you want to get straight to the heart of PSI and discover what you really think of people and what they think of you, then go straight to Chapter 8 of the Lexicon and follow the instructions. In minutes you can learn what it means if you think your best friend is a Bacon, Lettuce and Tomato sandwich.

Similarly, if you want to know your character through your choice of one of the Seven Deadly Sins, then refer to page 113 where all is revealed.

Alternatively, having entertained yourself by dipping here and there, you can take the PSI technique a lot further and use it properly in Compatibility Tests.

As you will discover, this book is intentionally humorous but it is not necessarily light-hearted. The strength of a technique which comprises Psychology, Slander and Intuition is that while it is very amusing it can also be alarmingly accurate.

THE PSI LEXICON

A guide to personality from Volvo Man
to Costa del Sol Woman

Introduction

The Lexicon which follows is the heart of this book. It was the great Swiss psychologist Jung who made modern man especially aware of symbols and their universal significance and power. They emerge from centuries of common experience and sink deep into the collective unconscious of the human mind. The experiences of life and death, dawning and darkening, birth and awakening, have been with us since the beginning of conscious experience. As they have invested life with meaning, so man has tried to capture them symbolically and express their meaning in metaphor. From cave drawings to magic circles, great poetry to music, humans have endeavoured to express and manage the mystery and power of what they know and feel.

Some of these symbols have a significance that is almost instinctive. The horror and fascination that a snake creates – its venomous beauty and legless, sinewy movements of great speed and silence – link power and evil together with dramatic force. It hardly needs the story of Temptation in the Garden of Eden to fix the snake for ever in western consciousness as the most potent sign of evil infiltration.

Where myth takes over from intuition need not concern us here. Symbols there are, and so they become powerful means of communication. Lions, giants, ogres, witches, wizards and hobgoblins populate the childhoods of all nations in one form or another. Behind the innocence of nursery rhymes night terrors may also lurk.

The greater facility we have for communicating, the more symbols and images become the shorthand of our lives. Advertising thrives on symbols; marketing seeks to create products that tap into unstated needs. Pop stars are packaged. Motor cars are endowed with qualities that have very little immediate relevance to getting from A to B. Our modern world is hugely symbolic, with most of the imagery manufactured for us.

In forming the Lexicon we have taken ten main classes of object from our modern lives – objects which have been invested with all kinds of meaning and symbolism by the cultural processes which informed us about them in the first place. An Australian's view of the pommie Brits; an Englishman's view of lecherous Italians; a Frenchman's view of the loud-speaking tourist; or a Chinaman's polite hostility to the white ghosts that colonised Hong Kong binds symbol and meaning together as a shorthand way of defining oneself and others. So too with inanimate objects. A Smallbone kitchen is as much a statement as an Aga surrounded by scrubbed pine. But there; I give my own symbols, metaphors and prejudices away. Perhaps there is a Smallbone/Aga kitchen. Now which of my friends would that be?

You will see from the Lexicon that we have taken:

1   Animals
2   Places
3   Drinks
4   Parts of the Body
5   Plants
6   Birds
7   Cars
8   Food
9   Materials
10   Cartoon Characters

as our main themes; and there are from five to nine in each category. To tell you more at this stage might spoil the fun. If the particular object to which you would compare yourself is not there, choose the one that resembles you the most. This is a bit of arm-twisting. Technically it's called forced choice. Psychologists do it in all kinds of assessments as a means of avoiding an infinite number of possible answers. See how it goes. We think you'll be surprised at the fit you get.

As in other popular self-assessment books – such as the widely translated 'Know Your Own Personality' by Eysenck and Wilson – what we want to do here is stimulate, amuse and inform from a sound base. We do not expect serious decisions to be made because of this book, but we hope it will provoke curiosity and serious thought. The applied psychologist in me really does believe that the complexity of people is the most worthwhile study there is. If this book awakes the cynic in you but leaves you surprised, we'll all be pleased.

Dr Paul Brown

1 ANIMALS

To reveal your opinion of yourself, your friends or your partners, ask yourself:

'If I/they were one of the following animals, which would they be?'

To reveal another person's opinion of you or someone else, or of themselves, ask them:

'If you/he/she or I was an animal, which of the following would they/I be?'

The choices:
- (a) Elephant
- (b) Horse
- (c) Mouse
- (d) Pig
- (e) Snake
- (f) Lion
- (g) Deer

1a Elephant

PSYCHOLOGY
Docile with tremendous strength; fierce in protecting young; legendary for loyalty and long life; capricious and liable to run amok. The elephant pulls great weights, bears huge loads on its shoulders but no one ever said, 'It's the straw that broke the elephant's back.' Remarkable memory, slow to anger, sometimes thought of as an endangered species. Alas, often wanted more for their treasure (tusks = money) than themselves. If male, powerful and in charge unless strength is ebbing and gone rogue. If female, endlessly patient and protective with a strong herd instinct.

SLANDER AND INTUITION
Now, before you burst into tears it doesn't necessarily mean you're fat. For instance, you could be grey and wrinkly or have a nose that hangs down to the ground. Alternatively, you may have been compared to the biggest animal on dry land because of your placid nature, delicate tread, outstanding memory or gigantic flapping ears. Whatever the reason for the comparison, yours is a considerable presence; you loom large in the lives of others. And they're always very careful to avoid treading in your droppings.

If you describe your partner as an Elephant, it may be time to move to a bigger flat. Either that or you're still irked because he/she remembers a certain indiscretion on New Year's Eve five years ago.

If you describe yourself as an Elephant, you are far more likely to have in mind the beast's robust yet gentle qualities, and you may be terribly good at moving large tree trunks with your nose.

1b Horse

PSYCHOLOGY

What a range of possibilities! Pygmy to shire horse in size; milk-float to cavalry charger for occupation. Nuzzling, responsive to firm handling, requires control and bringing into line. As a woman, like a filly; as a man – a stallion? Proud and independent but nevertheless loved and in service. White horses tend to have knights riding on them, the hoped-for object of a fair maiden's salvation.

SLANDER AND INTUITION

Potent, powerful, practical – the Horse is all of these things and more. Being described as a Horse means that you are looked upon with awe, admired for your grace and respected for your level-headedness. However, the Horse does not engender a great deal of affection. Indeed it often means that you are considered to be somewhat cool and aloof.

If you describe your partner as a Horse, you are almost certainly being dominated by them and treat them with a little too much respect. This usually means that you haven't been together for too long. But don't worry, the longer you share a bathroom, the more this admiration will wear off as horses have an alarming tendency to turn eventually into pigs (see *Pig*).

If you describe yourself as a Horse, you are displaying a despicable amount of self-confidence which is justifiable only if you happen to be a captain of industry or captain of the West Indies cricket team. If you're neither of these things, stop kidding yourself.

PS: If a Frenchman describes you as a Horse, be warned – he/she probably wants to eat you.

1c Mouse

PSYCHOLOGY

Shy, retiring but also a curious nuisance. At the Mad Hatter's Tea Party, Dormouse was somnolent. Harvest mice live busily through the summer day on other people's goodies. Scurrying can make people frightened. Almost as intrusive as a snake, running up skirts or trouser legs, but not nearly so repellent. Try Beatrix Potter for the Tale of Two Bad Mice. In the end they made amends. If male, perhaps a slight tendency to preen and be busy – a sleek Edwardian bank clerk. If female, mousy but busy.

SLANDER AND INTUITION

'Are you a man or a mouse?' The jibe is less than fatally wounding these days, and can only have stung at all during times of mass conscription or when men drew pistols at dawn. Few men (or women) object to being compared with a creature regularly caricatured as being cute and cheeky with big eyes and a pleasantly furry body. Mice are generally looked upon with great affection, especially if they are of petite dimensions, and are known for their unwillingness to do harm to others. Mind you, they can leave a nasty hole in your skirtings.

If you describe your partner as a Mouse, you are loving, gentle and protective towards them. However, if you're not careful you may fall into a (mouse) trap of over-protectiveness, constantly keeping a strong arm around someone you perceive as weak, small and unable to look after themselves. This is a mistake. Despite their quiet, defensive nature, Mice are clever, nimble and cunning and always give at least as good as they get.

If you describe yourself as a Mouse, take a look around. Are you living in someone else's shadow? It may be time to reassert yourself instead of leaving all your decisions to some big cheese who's apparently far stronger and more capable. Get out there and bite a few ankles.

1d Pig

PSYCHOLOGY

It's the hidden character underneath the obvious that counts. Pigs have had a hard time and a bad press. Pig sticking was a favourite sport for bored cavalry men in the colonies. Hunting wild boar commands high prices in Germany and is still macho in New Zealand. Suckling pig is a tender South Seas treat. But the character of pigs remains camouflaged. If male, and if tusked, powerful and fearsome. If female, fecund and protective to the point of eating the young in order to prevent harm coming to them! Definitely someone who deals in absolutes and sees things only in terms of black or white. Pigs of either sex make good truffle hunters – there's sensitivity in there somewhere.

SLANDER AND INTUITION

In the embarrassed silence that follows whenever a person is described as a Pig, some placatory soul always says, 'Of course, they're actually very clean animals. It's just their sties that are dirty.' Don't be taken in. Being described as a Pig can mean only one thing – you're a slob. It means you probably stub cigarettes out on your plate, leave the top off toothpaste tubes, cut your toenails in front of the television or at the dinner table. Shoe polish is alien to you, soap anathema, and the only job you can get is as a dermatologist's test-bed. But while you may be revolting to look at, you're also revoltingly happy. Pigs revel in their disgusting surroundings, indeed there is good reason to believe they hardly notice them, and they are warm, gregarious and friendly. Always first to the bar to get their round in, they often manage to carry as much as half of it back. If a Pig asks you to go out, accept because they make excellent company. Just be sure you're wearing overalls.

If you describe your partner as a Pig, you are a supremely patient individual who is happy to put up with sweaty socks on the bedroom floor in return for their affection.

If you describe yourself as a Pig, you obviously have a fairly low opinion of yourself, but one which is probably not shared by your friends. Stop wearing so many horizontal stripes and your ego will receive a substantial boost.

1e   Snake

PSYCHOLOGY
Initial, slimy impressions are misleading. Everything about the Snake resists comfortable attraction – there's no warmth and there's also the possibility of being crushed by the coils of a deathly embrace. If male, poisonous or at least insinuating. If female, slender, brilliantly coloured and fatally alluring.

SLANDER AND INTUITION
Possessed of a low, belly-scraping cunning, Snakes are experts in elementary psychology and basic hypnosis and therefore make extremely successful double-glazing salesmen or expert seducers of the opposite sex. In fact Snakes are among the most sexual creatures in the PSI jungle – and don't they know it! Describe someone as a Snake and they'll recognise the signals immediately, and it won't be long before you're inextricably entwined.

If you describe your partner as a Snake, you probably enjoy the delicious thrill of a dangerous liaison. Half of you is resigned to their Snake-like charms, while the other half fears the sting in the tail. Not one for dull predictability, you love the daily challenge posed by your deceptive, untrustworthy reptile. There is also the added benefit that your parents absolutely loathe the Snake in your life and therefore refuse to pop in on you unexpectedly.

If you describe yourself as a Snake, you are either being falsely modest or childishly crude. Neither is terribly attractive but this is precisely what we might expect from someone as wilfully duplicitous as you. You probably cheated at school, dated several partners at once in your teens and are now a multi-bigamist with a large family in each of the households you sold double-glazing to.

1f Lion

PSYCHOLOGY

Strong family bonds in an unselfconscious pride. Like Elephants, the male can become grizzled and cantankerous with age but otherwise portrays, as does the female, a natural superiority. In self-indulgent moments you actually enjoy being lionised – it wouldn't happen if you weren't substantial anyway, but it can be flattering. A Lioness almost matches her husband in speed, skill and capability but is also proud of his slightly superior masculinity and relies on him for protection. Born free and staying that way. A natural entrepreneur.

SLANDER AND INTUITION

So you've been described as a Lion and you're feeling pretty pleased with yourself. Well, unfortunately it must be admitted that you have every right to.

The Lion combines strength and beauty in a way that no other animal in the PSI kingdom can. You are seen as masterful, powerful and totally in control. The only minor drawback to being called a Lion is that you are also thought of as being rather frightening.

In future, try to do a little more purring and a little less growling.

If you describe your partner as a Lion, you have an excellent relationship which is filled with excitement and romance. You are sexually adventurous (you do it with the light on), you are emotionally compatible (you kiss with your eyes closed) and there is still a streak of mad jungle passion in your relationship (you do it with the light on, with your eyes closed, up trees).

If you describe yourself as a Lion, your character can be summed up in one word. Inadequate. You've managed to convince yourself that you are King of the Beasts, when in fact the only similarities between you and the real thing are that you have a big mouth and tend to doze off after large meals.

1g Deer

PSYCHOLOGY

Like Horses, not surprisingly, there's a huge range. From stags in rut to dewy-eyed Bambis (more recently given a bad press as bimbos). As a male, ready to fight and protect. As a young male, ready to challenge for supremacy and meanwhile have fun on the side when the old male isn't watching. Good market makers. At risk of being hunted both for the pleasure of the kill and for the mounting of the head. As female, male dominated, leggy, elegant, and perhaps what husbands have in mind while eulogising other men's wives. Can be domesticated and give milk if inclined to the more homespun variety described above. Very special to children at Christmas if of northern origin.

SLANDER AND INTUITION

With those big eyes, delicate features and velvety fur, who could fail to fall in love with the Deer? You are shy, sweet, pretty and defenceless, always bright and always prepared to think the best of others.

But be warned, being described as a Deer also has less innocent connotations. You are seen as a highly sexual creature with a beguiling naiveté that the more earthy animals find hard to resist. Luckily for you, the Deer is also extremely fast on its feet.

If you describe your partner as a Deer, your relationship is purely physical. You feel that your other half exists only to give you pleasure and you have no qualms about taking advantage. As a ravenous carnivore, you enjoy your position of dominance and power, and you are probably an extremely salacious person. Try taking a cold shower now and again, or better still, invest in a course of Bromide tablets. Pervert.

If you describe yourself as a Deer, you are one of those tiresome people who believes that they are just too nice for this nasty world. You probably go in for clothes with floral patterns and sandals that haven't been tested on animals.

2 PLACES

To reveal your opinion of yourself, your friends or your partners, ask yourself:

'If I/they were one of the following places, which would they be?'

To reveal another person's opinion of you or someone else, or of themselves, ask them:

'If you/he/she or I was a place, which of the following would they/I be?'

The choices:
- (a) Sydney
- (b) Barnsley
- (c) Beirut
- (d) Costa del Sol
- (e) New York
- (f) Monte Carlo
- (g) Kuala Lumpur
- (h) Brussels
- (i) Rio de Janeiro
- (j) Paris

2a Sydney

PSYCHOLOGY

You are likely to be known for the grand gestures – think of the Opera House and the Harbour Bridge. Definitely extroverted – sales on a global level and a lot more sophistication underneath than at first expected. Both male and female are cosmopolitan, cheerfully assertive and very much the future citizens of the world starting out from the Pacific basin. Paradoxically, the sophistication lacks a certain depth as yet but you're learning fast.

SLANDER AND INTUITION

Unless your name actually is Sydney (in which case the person who called you it is an unimaginative moron) then you should be extremely flattered by being described as this exciting Aussie city. You are a brash, go-getting trendsetter, full of ambition and new ideas.

There is one slight drawback in being a Sydney, and that is that you are seen as being just a little vulgar, but this lack of Old World charm is more than made up for by your New World energy and practicality.

If you describe your partner as Sydney, it's not quite such good news. There is no real closeness in your relationship, and you certainly do not feel that this is the 'big one'. You are simply ships that pass in the Harbour, so whatever you do, don't get too involved.

If you describe yourself as Sydney, you are desperately ambitious and you almost certainly believe that you are destined for great things. However, as a typical Sydney, you may lack the patience needed to get where you want to go. Best just to relax, and remember – no matter what happens, you'll always be big down under.

2b   Barnsley

PSYCHOLOGY

Either an accepter or an escaper. It is not recorded that Shakespeare, Keats or T. S. Eliot found Barnsley a source of inspiration though John Braine did even if he had to get away. This town is the antithesis of Sydney. The world depends upon its Barnsleys to keep it greased and clean. Forever. If male, Andy Capp but kinder. If female, Flo but not defeated.

SLANDER AND INTUITION

Of course, if you're a real Barnsley – down to earth, no nonsense, practical, honest and a bit grimy round the edges – being compared to this jewel of the north will be like chip fat off a ferret's back. And quite rightly so. Most people would much sooner choose a Barnsley than any number of unreliable Kingston-upon-Thames, Eastbournes or Tunbridge Wells.

You know where you are with a Barnsley, and you know where they are most of the time – either in the pub, pigeon loft or a front row seat at the wrestling.

Things Barnsleys Can Do: Unblock u-bends, mend bicycles, play football.

Things Barnsleys Can't Do: Identify wine at blind tastings, get past the bouncers at Stringfellows (Peter Stringfellow excepted), travel by coach without starting to sing.

If your partner describes you as Barnsley, you are obviously someone he/she can depend on. The danger is that you will become tediously reliable. Therefore, though it may be contrary to your nature to do so, it might be worth indulging in the odd romantic extravagance – a bunch of daffs, a night at the dogs, or a candlelit tripe dinner for two – just to make sure that your loved one doesn't decide to go off and twin with someone more daring and exotic. Like a Middlesbrough or Walsall.

If you describe yourself as Barnsley, you see yourself as one of life's dull plodders. And you probably are.

2c   Beirut

PSYCHOLOGY

Full of internal conflicts but of fine and perhaps noble origin. If male, unproductively at war on all fronts with loved ones, hoping the conflicts will get sorted out. If female, anxiously trying to survive and make the best of insurmountable odds; fed up with the mess men make of things but unable to do anything else but cope as best may be.

SLANDER AND INTUITION

It would be untrue to say that being described as Beirut is an altogether 'good thing'. In fact it's not a good thing at all. It's terrible.

As a Beirut person you are seen as not necessarily violent, but desperate. You are riddled with conflict, you're anxious, unpredictable, and unnerving. You have a knack of creating an unpleasant atmosphere and of saying the wrong thing at the wrong time. You are the sort of person who wears brown flares and has to have jokes explained again and again until they're no longer funny. You are the kind of person who tells jokes that weren't funny in the first place. You probably talk to yourself on public transport.

The next time you find yourself having a long conversation with a close friend, ask yourself this question: Is there anyone actually there?

If you describe your partner as Beirut, call a solicitor immediately, ask for a divorce and insist on a 'quickie'.

If you describe yourself as Beirut, call that psychiatrist you've been seeing all these years and demand your money back.

2d Costa del Sol

PSYCHOLOGY

Distinctly down-market Sydney. Unlike Beirut, where the leit-motif invokes high tragedy, the Costa del Sol has no nobility and alas no tragedy. Bathos rather than bathing predominates. Enforce-packaged jollity, cheap wine and chips are the ultimate in mass escapism, yet nothing ever really changes. You are trapped in limited horizons, trying to create an impression that fundamentally you are without the resources or the ambition to do so. If male, a spectator trying unsuccessfully to be a player. If female, gradually discovering there is no substance to the males. Essentially attracted by the profoundly unadventurous.

SLANDER AND INTUITION

Costa del Sols are life's cheerleaders. They're having a great time and they're going to make damn sure everybody else does too – whether they like it or not.

Endlessly cheery, always noisy, Costa del Sols are the first to dance, the first to take their clothes off and the first to be violently ill. Despite this, they're always the last to leave.

Navigating the party circuit on a sea of alcohol, they live on little cubes of cheese and pineapple, cold rice salad and French bread. They have such advanced digestive systems that they can even manage to drink the bottle of sweet Martini that nobody else ever seems to want.

Costas are the most sociable people on the planet, yet they have difficulty forming lasting relationships as only other Costas can keep up with their non-stop party lifestyle. If two Costas do happen to bump into each other at a party or club, it's unlikely that either will be able to remember the other's name or phone number the next morning.

If you describe your partner as the Costa del Sol, you probably admire their sunny disposition and boundless energy but wish they'd turn the hi-fi down a bit from time to time. You also find yourself wondering how on earth they can wear flip-flops in January.

If you describe yourself as the Costa del Sol, and you live in a block of flats, could we ask you to turn the hi-fi down a bit?

2e New York

PSYCHOLOGY

Tense, frenetic, oscillating between huge extremes; action-focused, self-seeking and believing that rudeness is an essential virtue. A fatal flaw is not being sure which battles are worth fighting, so a lot of time is spent battling unnecessarily. If male, assertive and opinionated but really very provincial. If female, uncertain whether the feminist route was worth it because it is not so much fun being a man after all.

SLANDER AND INTUITION

Being described as New York would suggest that you are glamorous, powerful, exciting and trendy. It conjures up a picture of a wheeler-dealer with a finger on the pulse and a taste for action. But before you rush out and buy your Wall Street striped shirt and braces, think of the other possibilities. Being a New York also suggests a brashness bordering on arrogance. It denotes rudeness and insensitivity as well as a certain seediness that isn't terribly attractive. In other words, far from being a Big Apple – you might just be a Big Lemon.

If you describe your partner as New York, look out, you're heading for danger. You see your other half as a high achiever who may be about to slip out of your grasp. You are over-awed by their success and you are afraid that you just don't have the stamina to keep up.

If you describe yourself as New York, your apparently high self-esteem has pretty dodgy foundations. You aspire to an exciting, up-market lifestyle, but deep down you feel that the kind of person you would like to be is very different from the dull, predictable person you really are.

2f   Monte Carlo

PSYCHOLOGY

The slightly faded charm that nevertheless manages a continuing influx of new money makes for compelling attractiveness. There is a slightly risqué element that looks more comfortable and gently roué with increasing age. It speaks of the fun that we had, not the losses we suffered. If male, self-assured but not quite world class. If female, happy enough to be swept along on a tide of easy fortune without having to struggle to get off. You don't find the fighting troops in Monte Carlo, it is the staff officers there.

SLANDER AND INTUITION

Monte Carlos love the good things in life. Theirs is a champagne and cigars existence, and never mind the expense. MCs are not necessarily well off, but the tedious irritation of poverty does not concern them. What really matters is how they look, where they go and who they mingle with. MCs always tear up the gas bill and never read those boring letters the bank manager will insist on sending. Being natural gamblers, they're always confident that something or someone will eventually come to the aid of their bank balance.

Because Monte Carlos devote so much time and energy to erecting a glittering façade, they can be somewhat superficial. They simply don't have the time to read books or newspapers (though they leaf through the magazines at the hairdressers) and the only television they watch is recorded episodes of 'Dallas' and 'Dynasty' which, in their eyes, are raw, gritty, fly-on-the-wall documentaries about corporate infighting.

If you describe your partner as Monte Carlo, you believe yourself to be their intellectual superior by a comfortable margin. This is possibly correct, but it is also likely that you envy their sociability, risqué lifestyle and glamorous appearance. You are probably an accountant and, if male, are almost certainly going bald.

If you describe yourself as Monte Carlo, it is unlikely that you are ever accused of being over-modest, despite having quite a lot to be modest about. You are something of a Walter Mitty figure fantasising about a lifestyle you have neither the means nor the style to achieve. Others may see you as less Monte Carlo, and more Milton Keynes.

2g   Kuala Lumpur

PSYCHOLOGY

The very special quality of being KL is that you can immediately recognise other KLs, even across a crowded room – hence MI6. People trying to go to Kuala Lumpur often end up somewhere else. If male, therefore, you exude an exotic quality but may not always fulfil your apparent promise. If female, you have a rather understated but nevertheless deeply passionate nature – the mystery of China gets mixed with the heat of India, and while both are subdued, both can be provoked.

SLANDER AND INTUITION

The one thing you *can* be certain of with Kuala Lumpur is that nobody actually knows where it is. And if you've been described as a Kuala, the same can be said about you.

You are a mystery wrapped in an enigma; a shadowy figure whose personality baffles and intrigues everyone around you. Communication is certainly not your strong point, and no one knows for sure what really lies beneath that cold, impenetrable exterior.

If you don't already work for MI6, give them a call.

If you describe your partner as Kuala Lumpur, the news is all bad. All that secrecy means there is something to hide, and knowing Kuala Lumpurs, it is almost certainly a secret love affair. You can't be certain, but create a tearful and embarrassing scene anyway, just in case.

If you describe yourself as Kuala Lumpur, you really *are* in trouble. You are either a Moonie, a spaced-out ageing hippie or one of those people who writes blurb for estate agents. Whichever it is, you have completely lost touch with reality.

2h Brussels

PSYCHOLOGY

It is difficult to be anything other than part of a vast international secretariat in Brussels. This huge civil service for the EEC reflects itself in caution, expense account living, and long-range planning that may never materialise anyway. You will undoubtedly have high verbal ability, probably in several languages, and be able to conceptualise and rationalise almost anything out of existence. Questions of the meaning of life leave you unmoved as the only way to survive is to ignore such fundamentally important questions. If male, highly political on everyone's behalf, including your own, and you're always at risk of finding yourself trapped in ever-decreasing circles. If female, bright, supportive, and with an awful sense of time passing by and what a waste it all is, yet living is better than going home. Not even friends take advantage of the fact that you are there for a holiday. The nagging sense that there is something wrong is best avoided.

SLANDER AND INTUITION

Have you ever been to Brussels? Think hard because it is just possible that you went there and then instantly forgot everything about the place, because it is almost universally recognised as *the most* boring city in the entire world.

As a Brussels person, you are so tedious to be with, so unremarkable, so spectacularly ordinary that people completely lose the will to live after just five minutes in your company. You have a steady job, an average-sized family, a moderate income, a modest semi and are of medium build. You go to Indian restaurants and order steak and chips. You clean your teeth after every meal. You never ever forget to fill in your cheque stubs. You jog. You know how your video works. Your favourite topic of conversation is how rapid developments in computer technology have revolutionised the world of book-keeping.

If you describe your partner as Brussels, you deserve a great deal of sympathy. You are living with a monster who will turn your relationship into an episode of 'Terry and June' unless you pack your bags immediately.

If you describe yourself as Brussels, all is not lost. All you have to do is give up your job, join a Jazz Funk band, get your hair cut into a Mohican and shave off your eyebrows. Then simply peel the 'Neighbourhood Watch' stickers off your windows and you may just become vaguely interesting.

2i Rio de Janeiro

PSYCHOLOGY
Here's masculinity and femininity thoroughly on display. As a male, might well be an up-and-coming intelligent boxer enjoying the glitz and the glamour and putting in a lot of hard work behind the scenes. If female, distinctly sassy.

SLANDER AND INTUITION
If the person describing you as Rio hasn't been there, then this is good news. They see you as exciting, glamorous, quick witted but easy-going.

On the other hand, if they have been to Rio, you'd better think twice. They could be suggesting that your exterior charm is largely at the expense of others, and that you are a taker rather than a giver who is prepared to party while those around you starve.

If you describe your partner as Rio, they are the Carnival in your life. They probably still make your pulse race, and their 'mañana' attitude to life makes your partnership pleasantly easy-going. Unfortunately, when 'mañana' finally comes, it's you who has to do all the washing, cleaning and apologising.

If you describe yourself as Rio, you have put honesty before modesty. You are convinced that Rio reflects your Latin charm, your passionate character, your love of life. In fact it merely shows that you are a little shallow, always ready to throw a wild party, but always quick to burst into tears when someone spills wine on the carpet.

2j   Paris

PSYCHOLOGY
Eternal mystery; elegant, whatever the age; never the comic and surprised that Australians can make films. You will ooze charm and display a world weariness from which you escape through creative intelligence. You are still puzzled that the last two World Wars reduced the manhood of France in the way that they did. However, grand concepts still inspire you and sophistication has not blunted patriotism in any form. As male, completely alluring to all females everywhere. As female, equally so vice versa.

SLANDER AND INTUITION
Stylish, elegant, charming. As Paris you love good food, good wine, good literature and creative parking. You are excellent company, but you do not suffer fools gladly and unfortunately you do not check too carefully that someone is a fool before you decide not to suffer them.

You are capable of breathtaking rudeness, but you have cultivated an impish smile that is designed to convince people that your arrogance is in fact simply confidence.

If you describe your partner as Paris, you've gone for age and experience rather than youth and virility. You respect your other half for their worldliness, cultured tastes, that streak of grey in the hair. But like all toy boys/girls, you can't resist doing that calculation in which you work out how old you will both be in twenty years, and the resulting vision of you spoon-feeding them soft boiled eggs and Wincarnis rather takes the edge off their Gallic charm.

If you describe yourself as Paris, you are the sort of person who uses the 'guide to good vintages' page in your Filofax when you order wine in restaurants. You fancy yourself as an arty, cosmopolitan, well-rounded sort of person who loves to enjoy life to the full. In fact, you simply eat and drink too much and you're not so much 'rounded' as obese.

3 DRINKS

To reveal your opinion of yourself, your friends or your partners, ask yourself:

'If I/they were one of the following drinks, which would they be?'

To reveal another person's opinion of you or someone else, or of themselves, ask them:

'If you/he/she or I was a drink, which of the following would they/I be?'

The choices:
(a) Snakebite
(b) 110° Proof Polish Pure Spirit
(c) A Full-bodied Claret
(d) Champagne
(e) Lager

3a   Snakebite

PSYCHOLOGY
If male, particularly good at office politics of a kind that hurt other people when they have the rug pulled out from under them. If female, likely to enjoy the kiss-and-tell side of life.

SLANDER AND INTUITION
Technically, a Snakebite is a harmless-sounding mixture of lager and cider. But publicans up and down the country know that, for some inexplicable reason, Snakebites are the recipe for disaster.

As a Snakebite person, you are an ugly incident just waiting to happen. You are violent, morose and aggressive, you have 'love' and 'hate' tattooed on your knuckles, you're on probation, you live in a caravan and own an unlicensed shotgun, you wear zip-up jumpers and your teeth are rotten. You pretend that you used to be in the SAS.

Everyone hates a Snakebite because they never know what it is going to do to them. One minute, you can be their best friend, they will put their arm round you and offer you a roll up. The next minute, they will decide for no reason that you are responsible for the break-up of their third marriage and threaten to kill you.

If you have been described as a Snakebite by someone, please be calm and try not to cause a scene. They're only taking the PSI.

If you describe your partner as a Snakebite, you are probably using it as grounds for divorce and quite right too.

If you describe yourself as a Snakebite, you're probably getting quite angry by now. But please, come down off the roof and let's talk about it.

3b 110° Proof Polish Pure Spirit

PSYCHOLOGY

There is an air of desperation, world weariness and existential gloom about you. The gaiety has a driven quality about it. You know that life is all turmoil underneath and essentially hopeless. If male, fatally attractive in a lugubrious way or at risk of becoming paranoid. If female, ever hopeful that the male will deliver the goods though knowing that really he never will. In your youth, fiery; later on, resigned.

SLANDER AND INTUITION

Polish Pure Spirits enjoy life with an enthusiasm few others can match. For them, life is for living and every minute is exploited to its maximum potential.

PPSs do everything to excess – especially drinking. They consume an enormous amount and they manage to drink so much *better* than everyone else. When they've had a skinful, PPSs don't become mournful and start talking about former lovers as a tiresome prelude to sudden unconsciousness.

The more *they* drink, the more energetic and cheerful they become and they're always keen to go on to a nightclub, even if it is 11 a.m. Many of these ebullient characters haven't even been home since the licensing laws changed and can often be seen trying to persuade unwilling office workers to join them in a lunchtime conga session.

Fortunately for them, PPSs never suffer from hang-overs but can rarely remember what happened the night before. Quite often they wake up to find they've sold their house for £5 or emigrated to Chad.

If you describe your partner as Polish Pure Spirit, you're making a desperate plea for a slightly more restrained approach to life, especially the wet bits of it. You have seen your other half only once in the past thirty days and that was during a brief visit to intensive care. You long for a quiet,

settled existence with someone less extreme, like Falstaff or
Charles II.

If you describe yourself as Polish Pure Spirit, you probably
sang your PSI choice while dancing naked on top of the washing machine.

3c   Full-bodied Claret

PSYCHOLOGY

Distinctly mellow. If male, may have some difficulty, however,
about being bottled up. It requires a lady of particular percep-
tiveness to unbottle you. If female, you may well have queenly
possibilities of fragrance.

SLANDER AND INTUITION

This has to be one of the best PSI descriptions in the book.
Being compared to wine is an honour only equalled by being
awarded an OBE or knighthood.

As a Claret, you have matured wonderfully. Granted,
you're not as young as you once were, but your wealth of
experience and knowledge of the ways of the world have made
you a fascinating conversationalist, a charming dinner guest
and a marvellous lover. You are unshakeable and unshock-
able, enjoying an enormous amount of respect from everyone
who knows you. You are almost certainly wealthy, but entirely discreet and unostentatious.

All in all you are a fully rounded human being who should
be enjoyed with a good cigar.

If you describe your partner as a Full-bodied Claret, you have
a love that's lasted and deepened with the years. You are
friends as much as lovers, and as much lovers now as you
were when you first met. You should be ashamed of yourself
at your age.

If you describe yourself as a Full-bodied Claret, you are anything but. Switch on the lights, blow out the candles, turn off

the romantic music. You are pompous, supercilious and boring, and someone should have told you that good wine doesn't come in plastic containers.

3d   Champagne

PSYCHOLOGY

The trouble is that there are all kinds of imitation too. Apparent ebullience may hide acidity and a sharpness that leaves a nasty aftertaste. If male, the more discreet the better. If female, perhaps too easily swept off your feet. Surrendering a slipper in order to drink champagne from it creates an uncomfortable lopsidedness.

SLANDER AND INTUITION

You really do have something to celebrate. As Champagne you are bubbly, lively, vivacious and fun, the perfect person to get any social gathering really fizzing.

Champagne people are only happy when they're in a crowd. They love to show off, they love to dress up, and they love to flirt. However, in spite of the fact that for you life is one long party, the people you meet can often become casualties of your happy-go-lucky lifestyle. Those who take you seriously can get hurt when you move on to your next admirer.

If you describe your partner as Champagne, you've only known each other for a few hours. How can you possibly call someone Champagne once you've seen them cutting their toenails or found one of their hairs stuck to the soap?

If you describe yourself as Champagne, you are labouring under the misapprehension that wearing brightly coloured clothes, drinking too much and making a fool of yourself in public makes you a 'fun' person. Either completely change your personality, or get a job in advertising, where you get paid for that sort of thing.

3e Lager

PSYCHOLOGY

Canned or bottled, neither are attractive epithets. If male, you may try hard to be different and distinguish yourself from the common herd, but in the end are a mass-consumption man. If female, likely to be of low alcohol strength and in consequence you are rather on the surface and safe.

SLANDER AND INTUITION

You're a real lads' lad or one of the girls and you're out to have a good time. A good time for you is an afternoon at the match (punch-up optional) or a night at a disco called Bonkers or Blazers or Roxy's or Foxy's, for Lagers are creatures who like to herd.

Both of these apparently dissimilar pastimes require the same careful planning. You are, after all, what you wear and you'd no more chant on the terraces without your Lacoste than you'd stand under the strobes without white stilettos.

When Lager man meets Lager woman medallions entwine and the result is nearly always matrimony and a home that looks like the world's smallest branch of MFI. Lagers have a narrow view of life and their interest in world affairs barely extends to the next borough. What matters to them is acquiring or upgrading their car, hi-fi or pit bull terrier.

Still, Lagers undoubtedly have fun and their lives are shadowed by just one niggling problem: drinking all that lager doesn't half make your jeans difficult to get into.

If you describe your partner as Lager, you see them as predictable and uninspiring. Whereas once he/she stood out in a crowd, now he/she appears rather ordinary, and every day you spend together seems exactly the same as the one before. It might be best for both of you if you were to try another drink in a different bar.

If you describe yourself as Lager, you are displaying the inspired lack of imagination which characterises the true Lager. But don't be bitter, this is a very mild criticism.

4   PARTS OF THE BODY

To reveal your opinion of yourself, your friends or your partners, ask yourself:

'If I/They were one of the following parts of the body, which would they be?'

To reveal another person's opinion of you or someone else, or of themselves, ask them:

'If you/he/she or I was parts of the body, which of the following would they/I be?'

The choices:

(a)   Feet
(b)   Hands
(c)   Head
(d)   Nipples
(e)   Genitalia

4a Feet

PSYCHOLOGY

Pedestrian is the essential characteristic. Nevertheless, take heart from being immensely valuable. If sometimes plodding, yet sometimes surprisingly graceful. Above every Foot there is the possibility of a well-turned ankle. If male, might be athletic and graceful or flat-footed. If female, remember the fate of Clementine and beware of driving ducklings anywhere.

SLANDER AND INTUITION

If you've been described as Feet, the best thing you can do is take your weight off them, take a seat and prepare yourself for the worst.

You are one of life's foot soldiers. You work hard, you're reliable, you do all that's expected of you and you do it well. Yet, no one, not a solitary person, ever thanks you for it. Due to the fact that you have almost no personality and nil charisma, people seem to forget that you even exist. You have one of those blank faces that blends into the background, you have one of those jobs that everyone has heard of but no one quite understands, you wear clothes that Ken Barlow would reject for being too dull. It is people like you who keep the world going. You organise bus timetables, you clear up the mess after pop concerts, and you write safety regulations for industrial equipment. In fact you deserve a medal for it. But don't hold your breath, because as a Foot, you are destined to spend you whole life being trodden on.

If you describe your partner as a Foot, there are difficult times ahead. You are showing signs of extreme boredom which could result in your taking a walk.

If you describe yourself as a Foot, then take heart, because a Foot who knows he/she is a Foot is very probably about to rebel. You've grown tired of being walked all over, and the best thing for you to do is kick off your shoes and have some fun.

4b   Hands

PSYCHOLOGY

You have the capacity to be extremely expressive and sensitive. There is nothing that you cannot do if you set your mind to it. Everything is within your grasp. If male, you have the capacity to be strong and true, though if you have compromised, your finer feelings may be slightly creepy. If female, you have the power to stir imagination and turn heads, especially with a little decorative art.

SLANDER AND INTUITION

The person who described you as Hands has said something in PSI-speak that they would never dare to say in any other way. Because hands mean only one thing: LOVE.

Hands are for holding, for shaking and for kissing, and as a hand you are seen as warm, sensitive, capable and caring. Your physical good looks are matched by your emotional equilibrium, and people seem to trust you always to make the right decision.

But as a Hand you must be extremely careful. All this love and adoration can be a great temptation, and you could soon find yourself twisting people's emotions around your little finger.

If you describe your partner as Hands, get married immediately. If you are already married, have children. If you've already got children, have some more because yours is the perfect relationship. You enjoy that rare mix of intellectual compatibility, mutual respect, total trust and rampant sexual attraction that makes most ordinary couples want to throw up.

PARTS OF THE BODY   37

If you describe yourself as Hands, you are what Americans would call a loving, giving, sharing human being who can honestly relate to themselves, and what the British would call a pompous git.

4c   Head

PSYCHOLOGY

The trouble with the Head is that it can be too easily separated from the Heart. You are likely to be well defended emotionally and more prone to philosophise than take action. If male, over-conscious of your superiority. If female, hoping that your feelings side is going to be released. Perhaps a Sleeping Beauty.

SLANDER AND INTUITION

Being a clever so-and-so, you're doubtless already aware that everyone thinks you're a bit of an egg-head. Of course, this doesn't necessarily mean that you're a top boffin. As Einstein probably said, everything's relative, and the intellectual capabilities of those around you should always be taken into account.

For example, if you're playing PSI in *The Sun's* editorial department, or the dressing room of a professional football club, being described as a brain-box is hardly cause for unbridled celebration.

If, on the other hand, you're currently knocking back the amontillado with a handful of Oxford dons, or half a dozen Cambridge emeriti – you're laughing. Play your cards right and you might invent a really useful household gadget or become the next Fred Housego.

If you describe your partner as a Head, you clearly admire their cerebral qualities and their intelligent, thoughtful approach to life. While yours may not be the most passionate of relationships, you're happy to curl up at night with a good bookworm.

If you describe yourself as a Head, you probably aren't one at all. Really intelligent people – like chess Grandmasters and University Challenge teams – are so immersed in their intellectual pursuits that they rarely give themselves a passing thought, as their clothes so graphically illustrate. Real Heads don't have time for anything as trivial as PSI.

4d   Nipples

PSYCHOLOGY
Sensitive qualities are not to be ignored. If male, rarely noticed yet would be missed if you were not around. If female, you enjoy being the focus of attention and very expressive.

SLANDER AND INTUITION
To be described as a Nipple is a very serious business. Indeed, only an immature moron with a schoolboy sense of humour would find it at all amusing.

Nipples are very loving people. They give generously, they sustain others weaker than themselves, they provide comfort to those in need. Nipples are calm people with a mature attitude to life, which means they can always be relied on to lift and support their friends. Lots of Nipples work for charity. The Salvation Army is full of Nipples. Go to a meeting of the Women's Institute or the Freemasons and you'll see Nipples everywhere.

The one problem with being called a Nipple is the muffled giggling that inevitably follows. Take no notice. Hold your head high and proclaim in a clear voice, 'I am a Nipple.'

If you describe your partner as a Nipple, two obvious points stand out. Number one is that you are very much in love, and number two is that you have the kind of lasting relationship that will never sag.

If you describe yourself as a Nipple, you are a very strange person indeed. You have an obsession with yourself that is extremely unhealthy and shouldn't be pandered to. Try getting a little more exercise and fresh air.

4e   Genitalia

PSYCHOLOGY

You may be a person who feels severely misunderstood yet at the same time surprised by your own wilfulness. Sometimes you feel quite out of control. It is probable that you later regret the action that you engage in, and wish you had said ten minutes ago the clever thing that has only just occurred to you. If male, at risk of being an intrusive sort of person. If female, impressive.

SLANDER AND INTUITION

No part of the body provokes such hysteria as the Genitalia. Throughout history they have been looked at by artists from every angle, probed by poets and intellectually fondled by philosophers.

The Genitalia are so fundamental to all of our existences that they have also thrown up a huge number of synonyms, euphemisms, common vulgarities and popular slang words. Therefore, being described as the Genitalia could mean one of two profoundly different things.

1. You're a very giving, highly creative and admirably generous person in whom the fire of existence burns strong and bright. You are passionate, and yet tender and gentle; dominant, yet somehow submissive; energy flows out of you into others, just as you receive energy from them. You are the crucible of creation. Yours is the pestle, yours is the mortar and, after a quick grind, the precious seed of life is created. You are Earth. You are God.

2. You're a fu ... [this section of the PSI book has been removed at the request of the Department of Public Prosecution. Readers are advised to use their imagination or visit a football match for further details].

If you describe your partner as Genitalia, you've just made everyone else in the room go very red. If you have to be so obvious, please confine such behaviour to the privacy of your own living room.

If you describe yourself as Genitalia, you have deliberately chosen what you believe to be the most insulting comparison. You really must stop abusing yourself like this.

5 PLANTS

To reveal your opinion of yourself, your friends or your partners, ask yourself:

'If I/they were one of the following plants, which would they be?'

To reveal another person's opinion of you or someone else, or of themselves, ask them:

'If you/he/she or I was a plant, which of the following would they/I be?'

The choices:
(a) Sunflower
(b) Venus Fly Trap
(c) Poison Ivy
(d) Weeping Willow
(e) Pansy
(f) Carnation
(g) Moss

5a Sunflower

PSYCHOLOGY

Sunflowers bring a great deal of joy to children who marvel at their superior height and smiling beauty. Even if drying up, there is a lot of life in the seeds. The danger is of being a nonentity and getting lost in a crowd of similar types. You are the sort of person upon whom M & S target their fashion wear. If male, enjoying the apparently superior status but with rather shallow roots, likely to move on from executive estate to executive estate as your career stays firmly under other people's control. If female, smiling but unsubtle – a nodding and fitting partner for your upward striving but unsubtle mate.

SLANDER AND INTUITION

The Sunflower dances merrily through life, laughing and smiling and spreading happiness wherever he/she goes. Dame Nature has equipped Sunflowers with huge mouths and gigantic white teeth and their grins can illuminate football matches in the event of floodlight failure.

Sunflowers can often be seen playing the guitar at progressive church services or entertaining geriatric wards at Christmas, and their apparently limitless capacity for happiness can be puzzling, or at times downright irritating, to those of us whose faces are frozen in a rictus of misery.

Sunflowers, however, are not always as robust as they seem, and they wilt quickly in the sharp frost of criticism. At such moments they retreat to their bedrooms where they hug the cuddly toys of their childhood.

If you describe your partner as a Sunflower, they are obviously the light of your life, bringing sunshine wherever there is rain, light where there is darkness. This is a very good thing, because it means you can go on being a cynical, glowering old so-and-so while your other half chats to people and parties and is nice to children and animals on your behalf.

If you describe yourself as a Sunflower, you think you are the brilliantly shining star at the centre of your universe. No party is quite the same without your presence and the world is a colder, less entertaining place when you're not there. At least that's what you believe. In truth, the only characteristic you share with the Sunflower is a very big head.

5b   Venus Fly Trap

PSYCHOLOGY

A passive aggressive character ready to pull the rug from under others and do them down. Unctuous to be attractive, heartless in trying to be effective. You need to feed off others yet curiously don't seem to get much further yourself. Might enjoy being a journalist for the *News of the World* with aspirations to *The Sun*; male or female, you're envious of Sunflowers.

SLANDER AND INTUITION

The Venus Fly Trap is a deadly predator which shamelessly feeds on others in order to reach its goals. Venus Fly Traps are ruthless in romance, using and abusing their hapless partners – who are attracted by the exotic scent of evil – before cruelly discarding them in favour of someone richer, more attractive or better connected.

VFTs leave a trail of broken lives and suicide attempts in their wake and gain sadistic pleasure from the harm they inflict on their victims. VFTs are often very successful in their professional lives, as they have few qualms about trampling all over their colleagues on the way to the top of the ladder. Fly Traps are totally uninterested in the needs of others and for this reason make excellent salespeople, being particularly good at flogging things that people don't want and will never have a use for, like electric gherkin toasters and portable telephones.

If you describe your partner as a Venus Fly Trap, drop this book and start running. You recognise the brooding malevolence in your, admittedly, highly attractive other half, but think you can control the situation. You can't. Sooner or later you'll join a long list of victims and be discarded in favour of someone else. Do it to them before they do it to you.

If you describe yourself as a Venus Fly Trap, you're not as green as you look. VFTs are so proud of their ability to ensnare others that they quite cheerfully reveal their true nature. You are very probably the real thing and should never be invited to play PSI again.

5c   Poison Ivy

PSYCHOLOGY

Symbiotic relationships support you and you manage to find other people who need you as much as you do them. While, occasionally, curiously good things come of it – like mistletoe from an oak tree – there is a slightly unreal, vapid quality around it. Unlike the true Ivy which, though it clings, also adorns, there is nothing beneficial coming from people of the Poison Ivy type. If male, the kind of politician that gives local government a bad name. If female, you will use what power you have, however insignificant, to interfere where you can. Both male and female forms protest they're trying to do good while actually doing a lot of harm.

SLANDER AND INTUITION

Unable to make much of an impression themselves, Poison Ivies live vicariously, clinging to the lives of others, feeding off the salacious gossip that is their sole reason for existence.

At school, PIs are teachers' narks, always ready to reveal who wrote that rhyme on the lavatory wall, or whereabouts their classmates are hiding and making themselves sick with cigarettes. As a result they are loathed by children and teachers alike and are regularly assaulted by both, which accounts for their poor posture in later years.

Ivies always get jobs in offices, the perennial hive of gossips. They enjoy the flickering, unnatural light and warmth of the photocopying room, where they can pick up new titbits, or pass on their own ruthlessly edited version of some recently received intelligence.

PIs rarely enjoy much success in the conventional sense. They are too busy envying and disparaging the achievements of others to do much themselves, and their unattractive nature hardly makes them eligible. Poison Ivies often end their years unattached, their bitter memories supplying insufficient nutrients to keep them blooming.

If you describe your partner as Poison Ivy, you are the trellis to which he/she clings. You have stayed faithful either out of a sense of pity or because the PI in your life has some compromising photographs of you that he/she has threatened to send to a national newspaper. Poison Ivies *can* be trained to grow into fairly respectable human beings, but if this is your aim take care and always wear protective clothes.

If you describe yourself as Poison Ivy, you're probably passing on a bit of gossip about yourself. Why don't you go and take a bath in Paraquat?

5d   Weeping Willow

PSYCHOLOGY

Slightly fey as fronds glint in the sunlight, there is nevertheless a destructively tenacious quality about you. You are really only safe among your own kind and a good way off from anything solid. Close to stronger, more powerful people your roots will intertwine with their foundations and risk cracking them with a sinewy toughness that is hidden among the drains. As a male, you might be the kind of butler who acts like a servant but sneakily controls the master. In personal matters you break confidences. As a female, you might well be in the less principled end of PR and believe that any publicity is better than none. Kiss-and-tell exposés are your idea of investigative journalism.

SLANDER AND INTUITION

Not quite as romantic as it sounds, unfortunately. If you really are a Weeping Willow, the complete character assassination which follows will leave you all trembly and teary for at least a fortnight.

Weeping Willows are what are colloquially known as 'Drama Queens'. You are highly strung, ridiculously sensitive and almost pathologically self-obsessed. You are probably painfully thin and almost certainly smoke eighty cigarettes a day. You bore people endlessly about your latest doomed relationship, phone friends in tears at 4 a.m. to tell them that one of your cats has been in a fight, and often faint in public. Whenever you meet anyone you consider to be a relatively close acquaintance, you race across the room to kiss them on both cheeks – much to everyone's embarrassment – but when they've gone you bitch about them for hours.

There is, however, one chink of light amidst all this gloom. You'd be great playing one of the minor roles in a failing soap opera.

If you describe your partner as a Weeping Willow, it's decision time. Do you continue to pander to their volatile swings of emotion, carry on buying the groceries for all those 'resting actors' who've taken up residence in your living room, and continue to adopt every stray animal in the area? Or do you do the sensible thing – and head for the hills?

If you describe yourself as a Weeping Willow, this is probably a cry for help which will, as usual, go unanswered and presage yet another of your tedious failed suicide bids, involving a warm bath, a blunt safety razor, three orange flavoured Vitamin C tablets and a carefully timed 'farewell' phone call.

5e Pansies

PSYCHOLOGY

There is an undeserved opprobrium attached to pansies. People can't quite work out whether they admire or despise you. On the one hand you do not seem quite robust enough for life; on the other hand you seem to have a certain allure, shady though it might be. If male, rather happier since the flower power movement than in the first half of this century. If female, sometimes wondering if being simply a blushing Violet might not be less demanding.

SLANDER AND INTUITION
Pansies are nice, delicate little things that always keep their sunny side up. They're fragile and fragrant and pretty as a picture, which is a bit of a shame, really.

In the overgrown jungle of life, the defenceless Pansy does not fare well. With their brightly coloured clothes, squeaky little voices and shy, unassuming manner, they are continually ignored and tend to get trodden on. At school, Pansies are always excused PE and, after failing even to sit any exams due to a nervous rash, they find themselves quiet little jobs in reference libraries or the less popular museums, where they know that no one will shout at them.

If you describe your partner as a Pansy, you sometimes wish, when you stagger home at 6 a.m., reeking of strong drink and covered in love bites, that just once they'd ask where the hell you've been, instead of making you a nice cup of Earl Grey. But alas, they never will and you'll have to be a saint if you're not to join the rest of the world in ritually taking advantage of them.

If you describe yourself as a Pansy, you are displaying typically Pansyish behaviour. Your self-deprecating description reveals that you are quite aware of what a great big Pansy you are, but you're much too frightened to do anything about it.

5f Carnation

PSYCHOLOGY
A Ritzy quality surrounds you. On the most plebeian level you will find racing at Kemptown the height of fashion. On the most sophisticated, you stand alone, a single stem in a

slender crystal vase with hopes that the sun will shine tomorrow or with memories of the way it was last night. Never seen in office clothes, your special quality is always to add a particular touch of style wherever you are, and it is always connected with enjoyment although an underlying sense of existential weariness pervades your continuous efforts to bloom. As a male, very much in the marketing department. As female, troubled that you might always be the bridesmaid.

SLANDER AND INTUITION

This must be the best PSI plant in the whole garden, a fragrant mixture of elegance and *joie de vivre* that simply cannot be matched.

The Carnation suggests special celebrations, 'the Best Day of Your Life', and glittering receptions. As a Carnation you are considered to be physically attractive and extremely romantic. If you're not a potential bride or groom, you're at the very least the Best Man or Chief Bridesmaid. It is tempting to try to inject a little vitriol into the description but unfortunately for the rest of us, the Carnation is practically flawless.

If you describe your partner as a Carnation, the first bloom of love is still in flower. You are probably one of those couples who regularly bore their friends with their wedding photographs or slides of the honeymoon. You also still kiss in public. Yeeeuch.

If you describe yourself as a Carnation, your ego is in serious need of deflation and there is one quick, simple way to do it. If he had been asked, Clark Gable would also have called himself a Carnation. Says it all, really.

5g Moss

PSYCHOLOGY

There are, nevertheless, moments when you appear to glisten and have cool, desirable qualities. In the company of brighter and sunnier people you might bring a calming, unobtrusive self. Mossy banks are typically where fairy queens rest a while

despite the risk of waking up to find an ass. Generally un-
welcome, there are rare exceptions which add to the quality
of stable environments. If male, aspiring to run the TUC. If
female, at risk of being trodden under foot.

SLANDER AND INTUITION

Moss isn't really a plant, but then you're not really a person –
you're more of a fact of life that the rest of us have to put up
with.

You inhabit wet, slimy places that don't get much light and
thrive on neglect and decay. Mosses are often slum tenement
landlords, money lenders or estate agents, or even all three.
They have dirty fingernails, green teeth and shiny trousers.
Their breath doesn't just smell, it is actually visible. They are
obsequious towards anyone with more power than they have
and are unreasonable bullies towards those they consider to
be their subordinates. A true Moss keeps his/her money in a
grimy tin under the bed and uses teabags at least seven times
before throwing them away.

If you describe your partner as Moss, scrape them off the brick-
worth of your life before they start to crack the cement. Better
still, report them to the Inland Revenue – they're bound to be
fiddling their taxes.

If you describe yourself as Moss, you suffer the worst of
both worlds. You not only *are* a Moss, you're aware that
you're a Moss so you hate yourself as much as everyone else
does. Take some of the money from under your bed and buy
yourself an uninhabited Scottish island. But give the sheep an
option to leave before you move there.

6 BIRDS

To reveal your opinion of yourself, your friends or your partners, ask yourself:

'If I/they were one of the following birds, which would they be?'

To reveal another person's opinion of you or someone else, or of themselves, ask them:

'If you/he/she or I was a bird, which of the following would they/I be?'

The choices:
(a) Chicken
(b) Eagle
(c) Sparrow
(d) Swan
(e) Vulture
(f) Ostrich
(g) Pigeon

6a Chicken

PSYCHOLOGY

The original bird-brain, pecking about and squawking away; getting broody, sometimes for no good reason at all, and quite likely to find yourself raising ducklings by mistake. Very confusing. If female, much of the above applies. If male, possibilities of being cock-of-the-walk and very pleased with yourself indeed. Fine feathers and a fair bit of strutting may make a jolly fine bird, occasionally bred for fighting.

SLANDER AND INTUITION

Scarcely birds at all nowadays (when did you last see one fly?), Chickens are just as likely to appear in a 'Convenience Foods' category. That's the thing about Chickens. They're fairly handy to have around, are nearly always available and won't burn a hole in your pocket.

But it's unlikely that a Chicken will ever set the world on fire. Don't expect any of these rather bland, colourless creatures to invent a top disease cure, write a best-selling novel or appear on Top of the Pops. They're content to scratch around in the chicken coop of life, and rarely bother to take control of their own destinies.

If you describe your partner as a Chicken, you obviously see them as a convenience rather than an essential. You get out of them what little you can, but rarely give anything other than the minimum amount of attention in return. Don't be surprised if this dismissive attitude backfires on you, for you could well discover that the Chicken in your life is having a bit on the side. Probably roast potatoes, peas and chipolata sausages.

If you describe yourself as a Chicken, approach the nearest mirror and tell yourself to get stuffed.

6b Eagle

PSYCHOLOGY

Like a Lion, but with the added dimension of the air –
hovering, swooping, stalking and far-seeing; the proudest bird
in armorial bearings. Self-sufficient loners of an unusually
high-achieving kind make Eagles – not disdainful, simply above
the common herd. As a man, proud, territorial and majestic.
As a woman, like a Lioness, a fitting mate for such a man.

SLANDER AND INTUITION

Domineering, dangerous, brave and bold. If you've just been
described as an Eagle go and do a lap of honour in the garden.
Far-sighted Eagles (in direct contrast to the spineless Chicken)
are always completely in control of their own lives, and exert
a powerful influence over the lives of others. These attractive,
graceful birds were nearly always head boy or girl at school,
and glide through life on a warm thermal of success.

On the debit side, Eagles tend to be rather fond of themselves (with reason, some might say) and they devote a great
deal of time to preening. They are also somewhat over-
aggressive on occasions and can be cruel and bullying towards those less well-equipped. Neither of these criticisms
is likely to dent an Eagle's solidly built self-confidence.

If you describe your partner as an Eagle, you probably live
your life in the shadow of someone you regard with a sense
of awe and wonder. There is also an element of fear in your
relationship and you suspect that your other half might one
day leave the nest and fly off elsewhere.

If you describe yourself as an Eagle, you are guilty either of
typically Eaglist vanity or typically Eaglist self-confidence.
Whichever it is, congratulations. You're a true Eagle.

6c Sparrow

PSYCHOLOGY

Cheeky, chirpy, cockney and apparently dull, but surprisingly
coloured beneath an apparently drab exterior, a great survivor

and enjoyer of life. If male, a small equivalent of the cockerel. Cock-sparrows enjoy strutting and having their hour upon the stage. If female, a slightly busier and more nimble equivalent of Lady BEFBT . . . (See Food).

SLANDER AND INTUITION

If you're playing PSI with a group of people, you've probably already got them eating out of your hand (or should it be the other way round?). Sparrows are always welcome wherever they go, and these chirpy, self-confident characters are at their best when they're performing for an audience or flirting with the opposite sex. Indeed, true happiness for a Sparrow is flirting with a member of the opposite sex in front of an audience.

Sparrows rarely get jobs as accountants or chartered surveyors. Their natural instinct is to buck the system, and they tend to make a very good living in a number of slightly shady ways – though nobody is ever sure quite what they are.

Possessed of boundless energy, Sparrows need three hours of sleep a day, never stop talking and can remember thousands of jokes at a time. Old people and children love Sparrows, as do all who can keep up with them.

If you describe your partner as a Sparrow, just make sure they appreciate the compliment. Yours is a rather exhausting relationship but you wouldn't change it for the world, even if you do occasionally feel that you're playing a supporting role in their non-stop performance.

If you describe yourself as a Sparrow, you probably hope that others will see it as proof of your innate modesty. In fact, everyone knows you're a born show-off, and you chose the description because you're aware it's attractive to the opposite sex.

6d Swan

PSYCHOLOGY

Serene and powerful, magnificent in flight, terrifying when roused to anger and ready to do GBH if necessary. Swans are high-level *mafia* as well as kings and, like the *mafioso*, are known to die from lead poisoning. Both types grub around in murky ponds. Swan children have doubts about their identity and are known as ugly ducklings. Swan parents know it will all work out in the end. Occasionally subject to the indignities of swan-upping, Swans have abandoned their truly regal status for habitations that bring them in touch with humans. Eagles never have. Mysterious though mournful – the Swan of Tuonela glides and glides. Leda, on the other hand, got ravished. Swans certainly span the range. If male, very elegant and certainly included in Royal Ascot. If female, rather like the Lioness and female Eagle, proud to be a fitting mate and fierce in defence of young. Both should beware of admiring their own reflections too much.

SLANDER AND INTUITION

The Swan is such an unusually fabulous creature to be compared to, that it can only be done justice in the form of a rather touching little poem. Ahem.

> The Swan is like no other bird,
> Noble pure and white.
> So graceful in the water,
> So elegant in flight.
>
> In PSI the Swan is King
> Of all the other birds.
> If means you are a master,
> Of art and song and words.
>
> But even though you seem serene,
> You are a little sad.
> Because beneath the surface,
> You're paddling like mad.

If you describe your partner as a Swan, you are in LOVE, with an enormous, gold inlaid, scrolled and be-cherubed capital 'L'. By some miracle, you've retained that lip trembling, dribble inducing feeling that you normally only get in the first few days of romance. There are two possible reasons for this.

1. You are incredibly naïve and stupid.
2. See 1.

If you describe yourself as a Swan, you are also in LOVE, with an enormous, gold inlaid, scrolled and be-cherubed capital 'L'. Unfortunately, this time it's you that you're in love with and you should be ashamed of yourself.

6e Vulture

PSYCHOLOGY
If male, a VAT inspector. If female, only wanting to inspect the corpse of a VAT inspector.

SLANDER AND INTUITION
Now dry your eyes and stop being so silly. Just because you've been compared to a Vulture, it doesn't necessarily mean that you are a repulsive, foul-smelling, morbid opportunist with a scraggy neck.

In fact, Vultures are extremely useful animals which do the dirty work that the rest of us wouldn't touch with a barge pole. So even though you are shunned and feared by those around you, just remember that deep down, your friends secretly admire you for the way in which you deal with your obvious personal problems, such as bad breath, terrible skin and extreme ugliness.

There are worse things to be described as in PSI, it's just that we can't think of one at the moment.

If you describe your partner as a Vulture, you are in serious trouble. There is a profound mistrust in your relationship, and you probably suspect that your other half is only hanging around to get the rich pickings from your vast estate when you finally fall off the perch.

If you describe yourself as a Vulture, stop tearing yourself apart and get on with the serious business of your life—tearing apart dead gazelles.

6f Ostrich

PSYCHOLOGY

Gawky, ruched up behind, and only variably in fashion. Oddly allied to the Snake through feather boas, there are nevertheless surprising qualities underneath. Required to run, you can move very fast indeed and have even been saddled and raced. It suggests, if you are male, that there are hidden qualities that a perceptive employer might well use if he or she is a lateral thinker about people. If female, it takes real power to produce such large and lovely eggs and rear vulnerable young safely – again qualities that are perhaps not so clear on the surface, lying hidden behind a slightly ungainly appearance. In both male and female quite a split between what is popular and apparent on the surface (feathers, subject to fashionable change) and attributes of some real substance underneath that are not very easily seen.

SLANDER AND INTUITION

Being compared to an Ostrich does *not* mean that you are the sort of short-sighted person who spends their life with their 'head in the sand'. Nothing so flattering.

It actually means that you are an extremely funny shape with a long neck, a round, oversized body, and long scraggy legs. More importantly, it means that you are looked on as something of an absurd bird. You are unpredictable, highly strung and prone to massive mood changes. The only small crumb of comfort is that your strange behaviour is looked on as amusing rather than disturbing.

If you describe your partner as an Ostrich, you are at that difficult stage in between thinking your partner is lovably eccentric and having them certified. If in doubt, have them certified.

If you describe yourself as an Ostrich, you are the clown who hides behind the mask of laughter in order to conceal your own innermost sadness. You a Chaplin, a Jacques Tati, a Jester. In short, you do lots of daft things to make people laugh but only succeed in making them think that you are a bit of a berk.

6g   Pigeon

PSYCHOLOGY

Pigeons live in lofts while Doves live in cotes – a much more up-market, Cotswold style of residence. Despite dirty city or wooded habitats, and being a thorough scavenger in both locations, immensely valuable as food or for flying bravely through hostilities.

It is a mystery how you can navigate such long distances so accurately – a quality shared by most of your feathered friends but only in your case harnessed to the domesticated, sporting or military pursuits of humans. Perhaps you are the ethereal equivalent of Dolphins and much more intelligent than has really been thought. Habits of an apparently routine kind, such as pecking, have also been harnessed to experimental psychology and you have done some remarkably good work in helping to develop spacecraft. There is rather more to you than just a bigger variety of Sparrow. If male, very ready to be territorial in pursuit of females. If female, surprisingly seductive.

SLANDER AND INTUITION

Common, boring, stupid and best kept cooped-up are the nicest things one can say about you. Your only true ability in life is to shit on people from a great height. On the bright side you are stupid enough to be trained into doing something useful like carrying messages (bike couriers, postmen, etc . . .), or entertaining thick American tourists in Trafalgar Square. Generally found in dirty cities, your company is unacceptable to any other bird (even Vultures), and though other Pigeons hang around with you they are likely to peck out your eyes at the first opportunity.

If you describe your partner as a Pigeon, you have either married for money and are waiting for them to die or have a domineering personality that enjoys keeping your possessions locked up with iron rings around their feet and only letting them out for short flights around the allotment.

If you describe yourself as a Pigeon, what can one say? Next time you answer this question – lie!

7   CARS

To reveal your opinion of yourself, your friends or your partners, ask yourself:

'If I/they were one of the following cars, which would they be?'

To reveal another person's opinion of you or someone else, or of themselves, ask them:

'If you/he/she or I was a car, which of the following would they/I be?'

The choices:
  (a)   Golf GTi
  (b)   Mercedes Benz
  (c)   Ferrari
  (d)   Volvo
  (e)   Ford Sierra
  (f)   Mini
  (g)   Rolls Royce
  (h)   Reliant Robin
  (i)   Transit Van

7a Golf GTi

PSYCHOLOGY

Germanic thoroughness and stylishness makes you a classic Anglo-Saxon type – clean-cut and comfortably energetic. Power is well available and well directed, with a great deal of stability underpinning it. As a male, high achiever though not entrepreneurial. As female, a very good girl chum and independent sports woman too.

SLANDER AND INTUITION

They may come in for a spot of gentle ribbing down at the wine bar every now and again, but secretly everyone admires the GTi.

They're professionally highly successful, but still manage to keep their feet firmly on the ground. They're fast-moving and upwardly-mobile, yet they always have time for family and friends and are trustworthy and reliable. They're quietly, almost subtly, attractive to both sexes, yet they are loyal and devoted partners.

The GTi is the sort who never misses a girl's night out or a drink with the boys, and at the end of the evening takes responsibility for making sure everyone gets home safely.

Whether they're a Rolls Royce or a Transit Van, everyone envies the GTi's apparently perfectly balanced existence.

If you describe your partner as a Golf GTi, yours is a stable and contented relationship. The GTi in your life provides the excitement and pace you relish as well as the devotion and dependability you crave.

If you describe yourself as a Golf GTi, you are merely trying to impress everyone with how terribly thrusting and successful you are. Why don't you just be quiet and let your Armani suit do the talking?

7b Mercedes Benz

PSYCHOLOGY

Immensely reliable and solid rather than fashionable. If male, even a little priggish. If female, more likely to enjoy sensible tweeds than bother about bikini line depilatories, but in every other sense definitely among the conservative crowd.

SLANDER AND INTUITION

No one doubts the efficiency of a Mercedes. Few would argue that they do their job well, are exceptionally reliable and smartly – if rather conservatively – turned out.

The problem is, they're just not terribly exciting. If a Mercedes buys a pet it's a goldfish, not a baby crocodile. If they work at advertising agencies they tend to be in accounts rather than the creative department. To other accountants they may well be rakish, swashbuckling ne'er-do-wells who ride roughshod over convention – but to the rest of us they're frankly dull.

When they take a break from totting up the debit columns, Mercs (they shudder at the abbreviation, and prefer 'Mr Benz') visit expensively exclusive clubs for an efficient, if cautious, round of golf, throw reasonably successful dinner parties at which there are more clients and colleagues than friends, and spend time with their spectacularly unprecocious children, all of whom are quite good at science.

If you describe your partner as a Mercedes Benz, you probably aren't complaining too loudly. You enjoy the material benefits that MBs accumulate and at least you know your solidly reliable other half isn't about to get drunk, rob a bank and fly out to Rio in the company of half a dozen Page Three Girls at the drop of a hat.

If you describe yourself as a Mercedes Benz, you have carefully gone for what you see as the most neutral choice. This type of behaviour is typical of MBs, who like to do things quietly and without anyone else noticing.

7c Ferrari

PSYCHOLOGY

Being attached to obvious rather than understated style, you are likely to buy your way into whatever you want in life and acquire it as a possession rather than develop it from within yourself. For the man who has piped underwater music in his swimming pool, a Ferrari near at hand completes the picture. The Italian image also implies a slight lack of substance which, paradoxically, is more apparent than real, because you always do deliver and prove to be highly reliable. If male, attracted by your own good looks and keen that others should notice you too. You are attracted by efficiency rather than mastery in women. If female, enjoying relationships that are supportive – even though you can give the appearance of independence: quite happy to slide over into the passenger's seat. You are fascinated by successful materialism in men.

SLANDER AND INTUITION

Describing someone as a Ferrari is a sure sign that somewhere in your relationship there's something sexual.

The key word with Ferraris is dominance. Ferrari people are seen as exciting, creative, dangerous and tantalisingly unobtainable. Paradoxically, describing someone as a Ferrari can also mean that in spite of the powerful physical attraction there is also a sense of strong personal dislike, as if the person mirrors something ugly in oneself. If you find yourself describing someone you have just met as a Ferrari, be warned – it'll end in tears.

If you describe your partner as a Ferrari, it suggests that you have a healthy physical relationship but that emotionally you feel a little intimidated by them. Affairs with Ferraris tend to be passionate but brief.

If you describe yourself as a Ferrari, you're a B Team Mike

Baldwin who buys *Mayfair* for the articles. Your over-inflated ego is probably out of all proportion to your physical dimensions.

7d   Volvo

PSYCHOLOGY

See the comments on page 96. There is something sneaky as well as wasteful and unnecessary in those permanently lit sidelights. Creating something so solid, staid and reliable, inured to almost all conditions of discomfort and yet having to advertise in such a discretely blatant way, makes it all seem un-British. Perhaps in Sweden it's the cars that don't have sidelights on that show up in the crowd – or perhaps the country is so controlled, with so little individuality, that everyone is required to have sidelights on anyway. This kind of person stands out, creates a slight sense of unease about their assumed superiority and yet beneath it all is worthwhile. If male, likely to do all the right things because they *ought* to be done rather than because it is *natural* to do them. If female, comfortably confident of one's own rightness and yet very sound too – English provincial middle class at its best and the future hope of both the Townswomen's Guild and the WI.

SLANDER AND INTUITION

Volvos can be summed up in one word: safe. Describing someone as a Volvo means you see them as stable, reliable, solid and consistent. It also suggests that you feel they have some sort of control over your actions. However, Volvos are benign rather than malevolent controllers. They are distant father figures whose authority is not feared or resented, merely tolerated.

If you describe your partner as a Volvo, beware! They are becoming part of the furniture. They have become safe and you are anxious to leave them behind at the lights for a more daring, racier model.

If you describe yourself as a Volvo – even worse. You desperately want a calm, controlled life but, in fact, things are beginning to get on top of you. You are probably suffering from too much pressure and are anxious to escape.

7e Ford Sierra

PSYCHOLOGY

Aspiration (and sometimes, feeling the strain, perspiration too) is the dominant characteristic here. Likely to be relatively young but, if older, at risk of reading about yourself every fortnight in *Private Eye*'s 'Great Bores of Today'. If male, trying to escape from middle management milieu. If female, worried about whether to have ruched curtains. Dame Edna might advise.

SLANDER AND INTUITION

Step into the world of Sierra and you're instantly in the land of the bland – consigned to the rear seat coat-hook of life.

Excitement in a Sierra means a spot of slip-streaming and a quick flash of the halogens in the outside lane, foot hard down because only a fool pays for his own petrol.

Other than that, it's middle lane life all the way, enjoying weekend jaunts with wife Tracey and children Darren and Danielle, and the comforting feel of a freshly pressed pair of Farahs against the well-developed accelerator thigh.

You'll never break down in a Sierra – at least not mechanically – and after all, it's not as if you bought the thing. It wouldn't be *your* choice. But it gets you from warehouse to customer and there's always the dream. The dream of that area manager's job at head office, 15K . . . and the Ford Granada.

If you describe your partner as a Sierra, you see them as reliable but perhaps rather dull. You would trust Sierra man to drive your kids to school but you wouldn't choose one to make up a foursome with Jerry Hall and Christie Brinkley. Sierra comparisons are deceptively barbed, implying few virtues and, worse still, no vices and suggesting a certain shapelessness that is one of the car's few noticeable characteristics.

If you describe yourself as a Sierra, it is time to carry out some hasty and critical self-appraisal. You are beginning to go unnoticed. You are no longer turning heads in the street and even your nearest and dearest now regards you as little more than a convenience. Suddenly you're getting stuck in life's middle management and you'd better do something about it or you'll become Volvo Man without the ackers or the obsession with safety. Still, it could conceivably be worse. You *could* be a Sierra Estate.

7f Mini

PSYCHOLOGY
Anchored firmly in the early sixties, there has been little development but nevertheless still essentially sound. You will come across people rather like yourself who seem a bit too flash (over-powered and under-braked) or who went the *nouveau riche* direction (Riley Elf) only to fail. If male, actually very sound though not a great inspirer of confidence. Might like sail-boarding rather than ocean racing. If female, smartly effective without being pushy – very good secretary bird.

SLANDER AND INTUITION
Being called a Mini should not be an ego-deflating experience. True, very short people are often called Minis in PSI but the comparison has much deeper connotations. Firstly it denotes a great deal of affection. It suggests a certain matiness which, although not sexual, is warmly felt. Minis are consistent, open and friendly, and usually inspire long-term friendships.

If you describe your partner as a Mini, this is not such good news. Your relationship lacks passion and you see your other half as a shoulder to cry on rather than as an object of desire.

If you describe yourself as a Mini, you lack self-esteem and perhaps feel that you are not achieving all you might. It can also be a symptom of thwarted ambition. However, you do at least perceive yourself as being a lovable failure.

7g   Rolls Royce

PSYCHOLOGY

Not sure whether you have really arrived or would like others to believe that you have. Nevertheless, you can and do demand certain levels of comfort and ease which give you the satisfaction of gliding and staying cool when others are getting the bumpy ride and finding the going tough. Real security lies in a Bentley Turbo but a Rolls will do on the way – and for many will do in any event. The older the Rolls, the more elegance; the younger, the more still to prove. If male, sometimes a bit too flash even if apparently well in control. If female, very elderly and waving comfortably out of the back of the car, chauffeur-driven through life, or preferring the slightly racier forms of drop-head and open style. Really secure Rolls Royce types generally leave it at home and drive the Saab or Quattro.

SLANDER AND INTUITION

Before you pat yourself on the back for being compared with 'the world's best car', think about what the comparison really implies. Rolls Royce stands for pompous authority, aloofness and late middle-aged flabbiness. Those who see you as a Rolls Royce see you as out of touch, oblivious and rather cold, although they may recognise a degree of dignity about you. People rarely fall in love with a Rolls Royce, though their company may be sought after for the benefits they can bring.

If you describe your partner as a Rolls Royce, you're attached to Sugar Daddy/Mummy. You don't love them for what they are, but for their power, prestige, breeding or money. What better basis could there be for a successful relationship?

If you describe yourself as a Rolls Royce, you've probably achieved a great deal and ambition is a thing of the past, while complacency is very much of the present. You see yourself as a person of taste and refinement who is happy to put the toys of childhood behind you in order to enjoy the finer things in life.

7h Reliant Robin

PSYCHOLOGY

The rather weaker child of what was once good yeoman stock. If young, still the possibility of change, though taste and discrimination are somewhat in doubt. However, you might not yet take yourself very seriously. If middle-aged, likely to have made compromises all the way down the line. If male, lower middle management and perhaps surprisingly belligerent in the name of lost causes like NHS porters. If female, very stuck in a social rut and routine without much expectation of change.

SLANDER AND INTUITION

Oh dear. Being compared to a Reliant Robin is never good news. It suggests that you are weak, slow, timid, old-fashioned and boring. What's more, you're seen as a harmless but slightly irritating nonentity. Those who call you a Reliant Robin seldom actually think about you, they probably have trouble even remembering your name. But when they are made aware of your miserable existence, they probably yawn or smile patronisingly. It might be a good idea to alter your image, change your friends or emigrate to Belgium where Reliants are much more easily accepted as ordinary citizens.

If your partner describes you as a Reliant Robin, leave them immediately.

If you describe yourself as a Reliant Robin, look on the bright side – at least you're not paying car tax.

7i Transit Van

PSYCHOLOGY

Utilitarian, ready to be hired for almost anything and sometimes getting into doubtful company. While lacking a certain style, it is not an issue that gives you any cause for concern. You are content with what and who you are, knowing you make things work better than they otherwise would. If slightly complacent and self-contented, you nevertheless deliver the goods on time. If male, a very good workhorse without any particular finesse.

SLANDER AND INTUITION

Transit Van people have the aroma of fried bacon on their breath and a rolled-up copy of *The Sun* in the back pocket of their trousers. You probably wouldn't want to share a flat, or a sandwich, with a Transit, but there are times when it's useful to have one you can call upon.

Immensely practical and very reliable, Transits can do all the things you can't, like repoint large buildings and touch spiders without screaming.

Transits care little for their appearance and often have ropey teeth and wear builder's bum jeans.

If your partner describes you as a Transit Van, yours is a relationship based purely on practical considerations. You need him/her to keep body and building alive and functioning.

If you describe yourself as a Transit Van, you see yourself less as a person and more as some sort of tool. You're never happier than when you're up to your knuckles in a spot of grouting.

8 FOOD

To reveal your opinion of yourself, your friends or your partners, ask yourself:

'If I/they were one of the following foods, which would they be?'

To reveal another person's opinion of you or someone else, or of themselves, ask them:

'If you/he/she or I was a food, which of the following would they/I be?'

The choices:

- (a) Bacon, Egg, Fried Bread, Tomatoes, Mushrooms, Chips, Two Slices of Bread and Butter and a Large Mug of Tea
- (b) A Single Lettuce Leaf
- (c) Lentil Bake with Mung Beans and Wholemeal Bread
- (d) A Ploughman's Lunch and a Half of Best Bitter
- (e) Escargots Followed by Steak Tartare Served with a Sprinkling of Lightly Steamed Mangetouts Served with a Chilled Glass of Macon Lugny '74
- (f) BLT on Brown with Mayo
- (g) Chinese Take-away

8a   Bacon, Egg, Fried Bread, Tomatoes, Mushrooms, Chips, Two Slices of Bread and Butter and a Large Mug of Tea

PSYCHOLOGY

Only the salt (of the earth) is missing. It can be up-market (British Rail, as was, on the Mancunian or the Cutler from Sheffield), in a northern sort of way, but is more to do with solidity and predictability than spice. Fantasies of devilled kidneys and kedgeree in chafing dishes on the sideboard are not part of this person's make-up – though if female, would be willing to be the housekeeper and learn; if male, would think he was getting above his station.

SLANDER AND INTUITION

Nearly everybody knows a Bacon, Egg, Fried Bread, Tomatoes, Mushrooms, Chips, Two Slices of Bread and Butter and a Large Mug of Tea. They stand out in a crowd because of their awe-inspiring ability to go out in the evening, drink 25 litres of red wine, then get up at 7 a.m. and breakfast on bacon, egg, fried bread, tomatoes, etc., etc.

Sturdy and reliable, with a tendency to call everyone 'mate', they're handy to have around in a crisis, or if a skin-head makes fun of your clothes – which is the same thing really.

BEFBTMCTSOBABAALMOTs are friendly, welcoming types who are always happy to share café tables and ketchup bottles with complete strangers. Some believe they have no control over their own destinies and are happy to surrender their fate to the benign indifference of the universe, in which case they are known as Bacon-and-Eggsistentialists.

If you describe your partner as Bacon, Egg, Fried Bread, Tomatoes, Mushrooms, Chips, Two Slices of Bread and Butter and a Large Mug of Tea, you probably long ago gave up any hope that they might one day be miraculously transformed into a Monte Carlo (see *Places*). Instead you love them for their honesty, loyalty and seemingly insatiable appetites.

If you describe youself as (see above), you are pleasantly modest and sound like a very good egg. Preferably fried but still nice and runny.

8b   A Single Lettuce Leaf

PSYCHOLOGY

The redeeming feature is that there are crisp forms as well as soggy forms. Almost always better dressed, SLLs wilt very readily and are always in support of more colourful or stronger flavoured characters. They also run a continuous risk of being shredded. In the worst cases they simply go to seed. The most energetic thing a Lettuce ever does is to bolt. If male, only the crisp variety will do. Might be charmingly homosexual. If female, similarly crisp and usually beautifully if somewhat trimly dressed. At risk of remaining a perpetual aunt, though smilingly so.

SLANDER AND INTUITION

You've been described as a Lettuce Leaf and you are just a little bit upset. But because you *are* a Lettuce Leaf, the last thing on earth you would do is let on, just in case it caused any kind of unpleasantness.

As a Lettuce Leaf you are painfully shy and timid, always first to say sorry when someone treads on *your* toe, and always last to complain about the three-day heavy metal glue-sniffing party going on next door. At discos you're not so much a wallflower as a floral pattern on the wallpaper.

If you describe your partner as a Lettuce Leaf, you are extremely unusual as most Lettuce Leaves don't have the courage to find a partner. Your description does, however, suggest that the relationship can't last and that you are already looking for something a little more filling.

If you describe yourself as a Lettuce Leaf, you are displaying the typical self-effacing modesty of the Lettuce, and your assessment of your personality is almost certainly accurate.

8c   Lentil Bake with Mung Beans and Wholemeal Bread

PSYCHOLOGY

This is a rather more concerned version of Bacon, Egg, Fried Bread, etc. Or at least, rather more intellectual. The concerns are stated, read about, sometimes written about and expressed in food but not very often acted upon unless a shift towards fanaticism takes place, which can be uncompromising. Introverted rather than extroverted and searching for like-minded supporters, quiet determination often gives way under the blandishments of increasing affluence and materialism. With advancing age, delightfully English dottiness of the truest kind. Completely reliable but difficult to get involved. If male, a gatherer rather than a hunter. If female, not so much a mover as a mother.

SLANDER AND INTUITION

Being compared to this particularly wholesome meal means that you are a disgustingly wholesome person.

With your garden flat in London's Muesli Belt, your 2CV and your 'Nuclear Power Nein Danke' stickers, you are the best friend the Earth ever had.

You never eat meat (although you may force yourself to eat fish), you don't drink or smoke, you never use aerosols, you spend hours in Sainsburys looking up E numbers and you haven't eaten white bread or sugar since before Glastonbury '78.

So why is it that you look awful and feel terrible? Better go and see the homœopath.

If you describe your partner as a Lentil Bake with Mung Beans and Wholemeal Bread, you probably discussed it with them for hours first, and after a quick group hug and primal screaming session, you decided it was the only description you could relate to. LBMBWBs tend to hang out in pairs.

If you describe yourself as a Lentil Bake with Mung Beans and Wholemeal Bread, it's better news. At least you know what you are and can laugh at yourself. Which is just as well really because everybody else does.

8d   A Ploughman's Lunch and a Half of Best Bitter

PSYCHOLOGY

A more active form of Lentil Bake . . . Essential characteristics are lost among the superficialities of life, collecting records and books by post, and hoping to become noticed as a member of the PTA, if not already a teacher. If male, straightforward, unsubtle and glad to have escaped from earlier wishes to go to the Costa del Sol. If female, wondering whether to abandon crimplene in favour of thermal underwear.

SLANDER AND INTUITION

If you've been described as a Ploughman's Lunch and a Half of Best, you probably haven't hung around to find out what it means anyway. Because you pride yourself on being industrious and active, and by now you'll have clambered into a hideously itchy pair of trousers or a tweed two-piece, pulled on some stout, well-polished brogues and gone off for a good brisk walk.

Having covered 30–40 miles at a pace even a Ghurka on war footing would object to, you 'repair' to a local 'hostelry', bid 'mine host' a 'hearty good morrow' and order a glass of his 'finest ale and a ploughman's lunch'.

Only a half of course, because you're not drinking to get drunk but to sample the fresh hops, yeast and barley skilfully blended in the traditional manner by a Swedish biochemist in some 21st-century computerised brewery in Widnes.

While 'quaffing', you consume a lump of dry bread, some stale cheese, a soft pickled onion and a garnish of limp lettuce. Satisfied that you've sampled the 'Best of British', you yomp back home for a stimulating evening listening to the 'wireless'.

If you describe your partner as a Ploughman's Lunch and a

Half of Best Bitter, you probably yearn for a little more excitement. Life can be as flat as a pint of real ale sometimes, and even your other half's interest in preserving the last remaining red telephone box in your area doesn't really provide the fizz you're looking for. It could be time to call last orders in the saloon bar of life before you wake up and find your personal tankard hanging next to the optics.

If you describe yourself as a Ploughman's Lunch and a Half of Best Bitter, you may have become rather set in your ways of late. A hobby could help: why not start a campaign to preserve British Telecom's attractive new aluminium telephone booths?

8e Escargots Followed by Steak Tartare Served with a Sprinkling of Lightly Steamed Mangetouts Served with a Chilled Glass of Macon Lugny '74

PSYCHOLOGY

Undoubtedly elegant but equally undoubtedly a carnivore. This person is either trying to convince that he is in control or really is – at first sight it is difficult to distinguish and supporting evidence is needed. Is removing snails from their shells symbolic of the fact that he only risks displaying morsels of himself and can, if necessary, be wholly and indifferently cruel? If a man, is everything just a little too contrived? Or have you really succeeded in discovering what elegance, implicitly, is about? If a woman, highly competitive and ready to take men on at their own game, and win, whilst staying thoroughly feminine.

SLANDER AND INTUITION

Goodness knows what you've done to deserve this, one of the most desirable PSIs in the book. Whoever compared you with this posh nosh is either (a) a close relative hoping to worm their way into your will; (b) a vile sycophant whom you're going to be interviewing for a job tomorrow morning; or (c) someone who desires your affection and/or body. (Note: (b) and (c) are not mutually exclusive.)

Escargots are rich, refined, elegant, stylish, understated, immensely attractive, popular, well presented and just a little decadent. Notable Escargots have included Noel Coward, the Duchess of Windsor and Cary Grant.

There now, doesn't that make you feel good?

If you describe your partner as Escargots Followed by Steak Tartare Served with a Sprinkling of Lightly Steamed Mangetouts, you are clearly madly in love. And if the comparison is anything like accurate, who can blame you?

If you describe yourself as Escargots Followed by Steak Tartare Served with a Sprinkling of Lightly Steamed Mangetouts, you either have a highly inflated opinion of yourself or a finely honed sense of irony. Score 10 points for the latter, deduct 1,000 points for the former.

8f   BLT on Brown with Mayo

PSYCHOLOGY

Stress problems here. It is difficult to get out of the race and enjoy the result – but then, if you are going to win you have got to be there winning: all the time. Relationships are likely to be suffering and you haven't time for managing anything other than your own immediate short-term goals. No matter how successful you are financially, it will begin to feel unprofitable. If a man, begin to think and feel like a woman. If a woman, why are you trying so hard not to be?

SLANDER AND INTUITION

For the uninitiated, a BLT is a Bacon, Lettuce and Tomato Sandwich, but a BLT person simply doesn't have time to use anything but abbreviations.

If you've been called a BLT it's because you are a whizz kid, a shooting star, the one to watch in the corporate structure. You work evenings and weekends, you never take a holiday and you always work through your lunch hour, which is why the BLT delivery from the local sandwich shop is right up your street. It's just a pity that you never have time to eat it.

If you describe your partner as a BLT, you're hitched to a career person who has very little time for unproductive things like romance and kissing and all that gooey stuff. Indeed, your other half is probably more in love with floppy discs than with you. Your best bet is either to ditch them, or get yourself employed as their secretary.

If you describe yourself as a BLT, it's just possible that you are kidding yourself a little bit. You see, *real* BLTs would never have time to do fun things like play PSI.

8g Chinese Take-away

PSYCHOLOGY

Depends whether authentic or high street substitute. As with all food, essentially the simpler the better. Trying to put on airs and graces will turn you into bland nothingness. If male, effectively hard working and unobtrusive. Didn't catch the shark but knew a good fin when he saw one. If female, even more unobtrusive and hard working.

SLANDER AND INTUITION

There are two possibilities: you are either *à la carte* or a set meal for two. Set meals are not good news, they are decidedly unadventurous. Despite there being several thousand items to choose from on the average Chinese menu, set meals always settle for being spare prawns cosseted in boring batter. They are impervious to the sweet and sour sauce supplied in a separate polystyrene container necessary to make them almost palatable to the rest of the world.

Set meals fool themselves with a false self-image: they believe Chinese Take-aways, like their characters, are broadminded and exotic. But sadly, the reality is confirmed every time you meet one: like the food itself, once they've gone you don't even know you've eaten.

À la cartes are fun sorts. Mixing and matching 67s with 49s, they make the most out of friends, food and Friday nights. Tribal in behaviour, they normally gather at the local watering hole before retiring, *en masse*, for their ritual battle with the chopsticks.

If you describe your partner as a Chinese Take-away, familiarity may be breeding contempt. Fond of them as you are, they aren't really satisfying your hunger. Perhaps it is time for them to swap the soy for something a little more spicy and take a slightly saucier attitude to life.

If you describe yourself as a Chinese Take-away, you're desperate for affection and long to be taken home and played with by long, thin wooden instruments. You probably have a lot to offer but lack an attractive 'shop front', often finding yourself left-over and thrown away in the morning.

9 MATERIALS

To reveal your opinion of yourself, your friends or your partners, ask yourself:

'If I/they were one of the following materials, which would they be?'

To reveal another person's opinion of you or someone else, or of themselves, ask them:

'If you/he/she or I was a material, which of the following would they/I be?'

The choices:

(a) Nylon
(b) Leather
(c) Pure Silk
(d) Cotton Wool
(e) Tweed
(f) Denim

9a   Nylon

PSYCHOLOGY

Very desirable on first contact, less so on prolonged acquaintance. Unlike Silk, there is nothing alluring in the Nylon individual. Covering beautiful legs, for instance, it is the beauty of the legs which enhance the Nylon rather than vice versa, while Silk would of itself increase the beauty. The synthetic quality leaves you firmly part of the bourgeoisie with rather snobbish pretensions. As female, beautifully turned out but lacking depth. As male, much the same: shallow relationships that leave surprising amounts of static behind.

SLANDER AND INTUITION

If you're a Nylon, the chances are that at this moment you're either being annoying, insulting, insensitive, dishonest or just downright boring.

Nylons are profoundly unattractive people, and to make matters worse they believe that the very opposite is true. Gazing into their own distorted mirror, they see themselves as urbane, witty and devastatingly desirable. Nylons are the ones who butt into other people's conversations at parties by just standing there and staring in an off-putting way at whoever is talking.

Very often, Nylons have to be painstakingly constructed before they can venture out into society and usually wear, attach or insert: false teeth, dangerously flammable wigs, tinted contact lenses, padding and corsetry of various kinds, umpteen different batteries and copious amounts of deodorant – though never quite enough for the person pressed against them on a crowded train.

If you describe your partner as Nylon, there can be little hope for the future of this relationship. It might be best if you were to bring the curtain down on this one and allow the man-made fibre in your life to go off and meet someone who really appreciates a good Nylon.

If you describe yourself as Nylon – good news! Real Nylons are entirely unself-critical. You must be a natural fabric after all.

9b Leather

PSYCHOLOGY

The hide that is tough can be substantially battered, and yet with a little TLC can be quickly restored to glowing again. Such a person is very resilient, infinitely useful, but needs the stimulus of being shaped or used by others really to come to life. In this sense likely to be a rather reactive individual but immensely trustworthy and reliable. If old, nevertheless with a warm beauty still apparent. If young, the appearance of fragility, like kid, belying the kind of toughness which is common to all leathers. For males, supple, long-lasting and immensely resilient if well fed. Not keen on fiery passion, but prefers rather deeper, sensuous contact. If female, perhaps working hard at remaining supple through bioenergetics or even something as graceful as ballet. A silky naturalness or a brightly dyed flashiness are both possible.

SLANDER AND INTUITION

When it comes to talking about the Leathers of this world, there's really only one other word worth mentioning, and you can rest assured that the word isn't dubbin. More than any other in the PSI vocabulary, Leather is the comparison that is laden most heavily with connotations of sex.

If you're described as Leather, you are seen as a highly sexual, deeply sensual and attractively threatening person who lives for the present and is eager to sample all that life can offer.

The opposite sex dreams about you at night, while your own sex probably says jealously nasty things behind your back. It can be lonely being a Leather; not many people feel strong enough to take on such a dangerously primal partner.

If you describe your partner as Leather, yours is a relationship which positively snarls with animal passion. Your other half will inevitably attract a lot of attention, so you must avoid falling prey to unwarranted jealousy, and you may require a course of vitamins to keep your strength up.

If you describe yourself as Leather, you believe that you have a strongly sexual image. In fact, there is a good chance that you are deluding yourself, and that everybody is laughing at your medallions down at the Over 60s Club.

9c   Pure Silk

PSYCHOLOGY

Eagles, Lions and Fine Claret share the perfection of Silk. There is a natural ease and beauty about you which is both long-lasting and apparently effortless. If male, you may be just a little too glossy to be real: may be lacking in depth. If female, infinitely desirable.

SLANDER AND INTUITION

Silks are the real smoothies of PSI's material world. They never put a tastefully shod foot wrong as they make their elegant way through life and they possess an effortless charm which, initially at least, makes them highly attractive to the opposite sex.

Silks always manage to have flattering photographs of themselves in their passports, can walk through rainstorms without getting wet and never ask for tomato ketchup in restaurants. This combination of tact and *savoir faire* means that Silks are often highly successful, usually in the diplomatic corps or as tobacco company spokespersons. They can, however, enjoy rather less success in their personal relationships. Their mirror-smooth veneer can become tiresome to those constantly exposed to its sheen, for whom a spot of dirt under the fingernails suddenly becomes somehow strangely attractive.

If you describe your partner as Pure Silk, you are delighted to have such a presentable, well-mannered companion by your side, and it must be comforting to know they won't suddenly start gatecrashing funerals to proposition the recently bereaved.

If you describe yourself as Pure Silk, you are almost certainly a man-made fibre. A true Silk is far too discreet to make such an immodest comparison.

9d Cotton Wool

PSYCHOLOGY

You will enjoy being cocooned and leading a padded existence. Never sure whether you are in the anteroom or engine room of life, and sometimes at risk of being depressed, you may turn out to be a person who acts most delicately or you may waste your life and simply be a swab. If male, over-curious. If female, trading too much on a baby-doll facility.

SLANDER AND INTUITION

Cotton Wools are the Peter Pans of PSI. Refusing to grow up and inhabit the nasty, mean, horridly beastly world of grown-ups, Cotton Wools think like children, act like children, dress like children (dungarees are *de rigueur*) and – most irritatingly – talk like them as well, especially when they're trying to be affectionate.

Cotton Wools think this stubborn refusal to clear the hurdle of puberty makes them deeply attractive to protective members of the opposite sex, and they attempt to enhance the image by wearing a lot of pink and pale blue and only using toiletries that have been distilled from Johnson's baby lotion.

Unfairly forced to meet the unreasonable demands of the adult world, they face many practical problems, not the least of which is their total unsuitability for any form of meaningful employment. For this reason they often get jobs in the theatre where they are assured of an abnormally high frequency of unwarranted kissing and hugging, and the kind of totally artificial affection they yearn for.

If you describe your partner as Cotton Wool, you have cravenly avoided more obviously pointed comparisons in favour of the amorphous cuddliness of Cotton Wool. The chances are that you now wish you hadn't.

If you describe yourself as Cotton Wool, you are somewhat muddle-headed and haven't totally grasped what this PSI business is all about. You chose Cotton Wool because it gets inserted into some extremely interesting places.

9e   Tweed

PSYCHOLOGY

If male, a little rough but immensely reliable and delighted to be thoroughly British. If female, good at being one of the boys: a little uncertain about your femininity or else deliberately disguising it.

SLANDER AND INTUITION

Robust and hearty, Tweeds firmly believe that true pleasure can only be achieved through pain – or by wearing itchy clothes at the very least.

Tweeds love long, exhausting walks but they absolutely adore it if these route marches can be into the teeth of a hurricane or during an icy downpour. This fondness for extreme discomfort and excruciating agony first manifests itself at school, where they enlist in hockey or rugby teams and waste no time in being walloped on the shins with a stick, or hit on the end of the nose by a fast-moving ball. Instead of crying, they just go slightly red in the cheeks and laugh hysterically.

Tweeds are usually quite wealthy – often through inheritance – but shun the comfortable desk job in the City. Instead they go into the demolition industry or become mediocre racing drivers in a bid to shatter every bone in their legs.

Tweeds are disquietingly frank about their bodies. They discuss their piles, warts and forthcoming operations quite freely with total strangers. In sports club dressing rooms (they go on playing their particular dangerous sport until they're at least 70) they have a disconcerting habit of standing around with no clothes on, openly looking at their team mates' private parts and flicking them with wet towels.

If you describe your partner as Tweed, you feel somewhat uncomfortable in your relationship, and you may be going through a rather abrasive period. You have an itch you cannot scratch and you need to take a careful look at what might be irritating you if you are to get over this rough patch.

If you describe yourself as Tweed, you believe yourself to be hard-wearing, practical, solidly put together and traditionally good-looking. In fact you're a boring old fogey whose only interest in life apart from yourself is the preservation of derelict churches.

9f   Denim

PSYCHOLOGY

Despite getting designed up from time to time, essentially good and strong without real aspirations, but seen in the most remarkable places. Both male and female likely to be completely classless and at ease anywhere, sometimes fitting much better in some places than in others. If at times a little overstretched and difficult to get on with, basically a good friend. Both male and female delightfully androgynous.

SLANDER AND INTUITION

A TV commercial of the late seventies used to proclaim that Denim was for the person who didn't have to try too hard. Lucky old you, it's absolutely true.

Denims are trendy without being fashion victims. They're sexy without being obvious. They're tough without being hard. As a Denim you have a youthful outlook on life, you're fun to be with but you also have a serious side which makes you practical and principled.

You are one of those sickening people who can eat anything and never put on weight. You have green fingers, animals like you and children stop crying when you pick them up. You're good at sport but don't practise, you get spotted by top film directors who shoot you on location in Italy. Everyone genuinely admires you. However, they also secretly want to murder you – and who can blame them?

If you describe your partner as Denim, good for you. You're stuck with Mr or Ms Perfect and you've avoided the temptation of indulging in an irrational and unreasonable outburst. It must be love.

If you describe yourself as Denim, you're broken the unwritten rule of Denimage. You're trying too hard.

10 CARTOON CHARACTERS

To reveal your opinion of yourself, your friends or your partners, ask yourself:

'If I/they were one of the following cartoon characters, which would they be?'

To reveal another person's opinion of you or someone else, or of themselves, ask them:

'If you/he/she or I was a cartoon character, which of the following would they/I be?'

The choices:
(a) Cruella de Ville
(b) Snow White
(c) Bugs Bunny
(d) Mr Magoo
(e) Fred Flintstone
(f) Popeye
(g) Dumbo

10a Cruella de Ville

PSYCHOLOGY

As a woman, there is nothing about you you will not use to further your own ends. More sociable than the typical witch and not at all interested in joining covens or anything else, you operate as a loner and are fatally attractive to men. As a man, you must be in drag.

SLANDER AND INTUITION

Genuine Cruellas will purr with delight at being so accurately identified. They adore the vampish dalmatian-napper's, sado-erotic image and would probably like to whip a close friend or small furry animal out of sheer gratitude.

Cruellas are happiest when they're humiliating waiters, shop assistants or their colleagues. Yet even for those of us who cower at their stalking approach, they can be profoundly attractive – particularly to anyone who collects pictures of Edwina Currie or is thinking of having their nipples pierced.

Cruellas are always expensively and stylishly dressed, wear perfume or aftershave that could stun a rhino at 50 yards, and eat an unhealthy amount of red meat.

If you describe your partner as Cruella de Ville, you are either very brave or totally in thrall to your hypnotic other half. Life for you will rarely be dull, but to avoid any unpleasant surprises never buy your Cruella a puppy for a birthday present.

If you describe yourself as a Cruella de Ville, it is probably wishful thinking. Have you thought about amateur dramatics as an outlet for your unfulfilled fantasies of dominance?

10b Snow White

PSYCHOLOGY

Archetypically tender but firm, able to call for everything protective in a man but still capable of mothering him too: a very complex yet apparently innocent personality. For you very little is out of place, untidy or disorganised – not that you are obsessional but the way things look on the surface matters a great deal. You are also capable of turning your own optimism into making everybody else believe everything is really all right. If male, very rare. Might turn out to be another Keats, perhaps not a Shelley and certainly not a Byron. Peter Pan qualities are around that Rupert Brooke would have recognised.

SLANDER AND INTUITION

Think of Maureen O'Hara, think of the young Judy Garland, think of at least some of the Nolans and you've personified Snow White.

A Snow White is fresh of face and white of tooth, has a voice like a babbling brook and rarely suffers from flatulence. All in all, it's a pretty boring package, but there's more to SWs than a syrupy sweetness and a fondness for community singing.

If you've just been described as the fairest of them all, you may well be the object of a less than innocent desire. Your unflawed purity – whether imagined or not – is extremely attractive and your apparent willingness to clamber into the first dwarf's bed you come across does nothing to diminish your allure.

If you describe your partner as Snow White, you love them for their delicacy, serenity and exacting personal hygiene standards. However, there are occasions when you would not object to a spot of smut creeping into the relationship.

If you describe yourself as Snow White, don't hold your breath waiting for Prince Charming to snap you up – it's unlikely he'd be able to put up with your smug self-satisfaction. You might do well to let your hair down once in a while and make someone grumpy feel very happy.

10c   Bugs Bunny

PSYCHOLOGY

The product of wonderfully irresponsible fecundity. If male, total confusion of action with direction, but wild optimism conquers all. If female, likely to be a hint of sadness around as it's not possible to sustain all that activity all the time. Bugs Bunny is a close relative of the mad March Hare; but the madness is of a cheerful and manic rather than melancholic kind.

SLANDER AND INTUITION

The hyperactive Bugs Bunnies are whirlwinds of undirected energy. They often grow up to become popular stand-up comedians, or make a fortune selling china from a stall in the market.

As babies, Bugs Bunnies rarely sleep and if they are a first child, exhausted parents usually ensure they are the only one. At school, teachers demand danger money merely to enter a classroom with a single Bugs in it. They know they will be instantly assaulted by any number of rabbit-inspired jokes involving buckets of water, drawing pins, electromagnets and thermonuclear warheads.

BBs spend half of their time inventing ingenious ways to get into trouble, and the rest formulating even more elaborate escape routes. However, they are not malicious creatures and those who escape serious injury are highly attracted to the cocksure charm of the vivacious Bugs.

If you describe your partner as Bugs Bunny, you probably barely have the energy left to turn this page. Life with a Bugs Bunny is far from restful but you are unlikely to find yourself getting bored. To avoid merely being pulled along in the slipstream of your partner's frantic lifestyle, make some effort to bring them under control from time to time, preferably using the carrot rather than the stick.

If you describe yourself as Bugs Bunny, you admire the adroit manner in which you manage to worm your way out of difficult, dangerous or embarrassing situations. *Note*: The PSI board game will put this ability to its most severe test.

10d Mr Magoo

PSYCHOLOGY
If male, exasperating. If female, equally so.

SLANDER AND INTUITION
As a Magoo, you are a kind of absent-minded professor without the Ph.D. You are a bumbling, shambling figure who is so caught up in your own little world that you are a danger not only to yourself but also to everyone around you.

You're an expert at driving tests because you've taken so many. You've been fired from hundreds of jobs for your terrible timekeeping, and you've only avoided fatal accidents, penury or worse due to the infinite patience of your friends; because in spite of everything, everyone loves a Magoo, and there is always someone on hand to pick up the pieces when you crash into one of life's carefully constructed crockery displays.

If you describe your partner as a Mr Magoo, you have the patience of a Saint and the sweet temper of an Angel. You have changed your life to accommodate your other half's unpredictable eccentricities, and you're prepared to take on the world to protect them from grim reality. In the end, the only reward you can expect is a shrug and an uncomprehending smile.

If you describe yourself as a Mr Magoo, you lack the total detachment of a true Magoo, because at least you can see what you are really like. Bona fide Magoos think they're Merlin, or the Lone Ranger or even Superman. However, you are at least partially out of touch with reality, and your condition is best described as 'Semi-Detached'.

10e   Fred Flintsone

PSYCHOLOGY

You have at least escaped being a Lager. There is a warmth and individuality about you which is valued by everyone who knows you. If male, the best neighbour ever. If female, an incipient Earth Mother or leader of cub pack.

SLANDER AND INTUITION

Unless you are planning to become a fashion model or a mean and moody pop star, being described as Fred Flintstone is pretty flattering.

Amongst your friends, your name is often prefixed with 'good old . . .' You are a brick, 'one of the best', salt of the earth, one of the boys. You are never slow to get a round in, always first to know 'the joke that's doing the rounds' about the latest natural disaster, and at parties you can usually be found competing with a prop forward in the 'balancing full pints of beer on your nose' competition. You eat and drink too much because you love everything, and you greet old friends by punching them a little too hard on the upper arm.

Despite your almost universal popularity, the drawback with being an FF is that people don't exactly rate you as the next Einstein.

If you describe your partner as a Fred Flintstone, you've resigned yourself to the fact that the thing you wake up to next morning will always be that big, always have smelly feet, and will always snore that loudly. But all of this is more than made up for when they give you one of their great big warm cuddles.

If you describe yourself as a Fred Flintstone, congratulations. You are a genuine, unpretentious, down-to-earth, good-natured slob.

Deloitte.

IT'S JUST

THOUGHT

07.07.
20

e, and keen on pumping iron, small-
As male, an unsubtle good guy. As
Olive Oyl and good at setting up
n which you can't really decide be-
you and will go through anything
ly wants you because he's jeal-
there but wouldn't know what to
u.

S. ... UITION

On... ...u can say about Popeyes, they're not wishy-
wash... ...d if this is how you've been described, then puff
out your chest, puff on your pipe and give yourself a hearty
slap on the back.

From your jaunty angled hat to your thick-soled boots,
you're a brash, no-nonsense character who stands up for
what's right against all the odds. You're not exactly Cary
Grant when it comes to charm, and you can't be doing with
politeness or sophistication. Because you're a Popeye, you
don't need to be told that you shouldn't change a thing because people like you for what you are.

If you describe your partner as a Popeye, you've grown used
to their endearing habit of giving you a rib-crunching bear
hug when they come home from work. You tolerate their
smelly socks and their pneumatic drill snores, but how much
longer can you put up with kissing them when they've got
spinach on their teeth? Probably forever, because once you've
loved a Popeye, no one else will do.

If you describe yourself as a Popeye, you may be mistaking
your strength of arm for strength of character. Anyone who
thinks they're a Popeye is probably more of a Bluto.

10g   Dumbo

PSYCHOLOGY

There is a certain lovable quality about you. Occupationally you might aspire to own your own dry cleaning shop or car valeting compound – those powerful suction cleaning hoses feel familiar. Substantially removed from real elephants yet feeling a distant affinity and trailing clouds of glory whence you came, aspirations are to own a Ford Sierra. If male, it might be worth getting your name on the list of a casting agent who wants bit parts for advertising commercials – the sort of Roman soldier in the crowd whose legs are cut out from under him by Boadicea because he didn't know that she preferred to be called Boudicca. If female, still making up your mind whether or not to attend Weight Watchers.

SLANDER AND INTUITION

If you're a Dumbo, you may be having problems reading this, and the best thing you can do is give up now and try a bit of colouring in. But if you're determined to persist, here goes.

You're thick, you're dim, not terribly bright, a clod, a dolt, a donkey. At school you were probably spotted early and spent a lot of time gardening. When you start new jobs, you're invariably sent out to get a new bubble for the spirit level, or you're sent to the fire station to get a refill for the extinguisher. Your verandah-like forehead, big ears and drooping bottom lip mean that you can be spotted as an under-achiever at a hundred paces. The lollipop lady knows your first name. You have acne and a plaster over one lens of your spectacles. Your trousers are four inches too short.

There is only one good thing about being a Dumbo. You're too stupid to realise how stupid you are.

If you describe your partner as a Dumbo, you mistook their silence and their blank expression for a smouldering and attractive moodiness. And now that you're discovered the truth there is only one solution. Tie them to a sapling by the side of the motorway and get back in the fast lane.

If you describe yourself as a Dumbo, you can't be. A true Dumbo wouldn't understand the question.

PSI AND ITS DEVELOPMENT

In all the academic arguments there are about what personality *is*, there are equally extensive, not to say fierce, arguments about how it might be measured or made objective in some way. After all, we all seem to have it. Yet it's very elusive. Try sitting in on an executive selection meeting, even at the very highest level of a boardroom appointment, and listen to how *little* agreement there often is about the candidate's personality. It's as if all the capable people striving to make a decision are using private frames of reference in looking at the other person. Indeed, that's exactly what they are doing

Psychological science has not yet established a universally agreed set of concepts as the basis for understanding personality. Things are more advanced than for, say, wine tasters, where the power of description allied to an acutely sensitive palate is all. But they are not so advanced as in the physical sciences, where there is at least some agreement on common units of measurement and where the physical and chemical properties of products can be experimentally controlled, understood and verified. Even so, disasters happen. When that beautiful aeroplane, the Comet, fell out of the sky into the sea near Rome, problems of metal fatigue as a consequence of high-speed flying began to be understood. When the Challenger disaster caused America to abandon its manned space flight programme until the technical problems were overcome, the minutiae of engineering endeavour became newsworthy worldwide. When President Nixon fell from grace, his going was unmarked by exhaustive enquiry into his personality structure to see whether lessons could be learned. A presidential candidate's tax returns or brief encounter with a sexy threat to his marital stability are more likely to be the units of measurement upon which electoral decisions are made. Taxation and temptation fit within common frames of reference and are convenient ways of ignoring more complex and more subtle issues for which there are as yet no certainties.

And yet we all *do* live out of our subjective certainties of other people – our private understandings which define our reactions to them, our predictions of them, and our hopes for them. We ignore the personalities of others at our peril – it is, after all, what makes them *people*! So there must be *something* in this personality business, if only we could get at it.

Which takes us back to the measuring problem. Two broadly different approaches are known. One sets out to measure people on scales. Introversion/extroversion is one very well-known scale or dimension of personality, and there are many others which have been described. In this way of thinking about personality, an individual's uniqueness is defined by the uniqueness of how all the points on a number of essentially independent dimensions of personality might combine. It is easy to see how individuals will be more or less like other individuals depending upon the similarity of their scores along various dimensions. This kind of personality assessment relies very much on *norms* – typical scores for defined groups, and how any one person fits against known score patterns.

But there is an alternative, quite different way of trying to understand another person. It relies not so much on measuring scales as on trying to clarify the *concepts* that another person uses. What are the *meanings* that a person gives to his or her experience?

This could take us into very deep philosophical waters. For fear of drowning we shall avoid them, except to note that in everyday, ordinary existence we all attribute qualities to objects and people as a way of making them understood and significant to us. The vehicle by which we express that significance is language, and words are the units of language. Lest *every* philosopher in the land says, 'How could you be so simplistic?', I remind you, dear reader, that I argue the case of the common, simple person who gets on with life and language and enjoys them. The complexity of life requires a language to make sense of it. Language and the words therein enlarge our sense of life.

In the world of PSI, instead of *describing* other people – even your closest friend sitting next to you – by using those common descriptive words called adjectives, you must tap into the collection of nouns sculling around your head which are the signifiers of your world. The way you name things is the way you are. The names that you attach to other people is the way they are. The fun of PSI is that your descriptions of others have to be based exclusively on the names you give them (or the names you call them!) and the power of association. A Volvo may be slightly staid even if immensely reliable, but what about those little sidelights that always let you know it's coming up from behind and going to overtake you like a tank. I have one friend who is *infuriated* by those little lights in her rearview mirror. They compel her to accelerate away or mutter imprecations of the harm she would do to the offending driver if she could. It's always a 'he'; wild peculiarities are attached to any woman driving such a machine. My friend doesn't like men who appear sneaky. She thinks Volvos sneak up from behind and *worry* her with their little lights; switched on whatever the weather. It also seems to her to be *wasteful* and *unnecessary* and she reminisces about switching off the lights during the war when she was a child. What a crowd of associations! How affronted! Beneath a staid exterior there lurks . . . well, never mind. I hope we remain friends.

THE PSI TESTS

SECTION ONE: ASPECTS OF PERSONALITY

One of the interesting facets that developed from the research by Dr James Thomson and Margaret Ballard is that the way people answered certain PSI questions corresponded statistically to how they answered questions in tests connected with personality and style.

Thus while the following test seems to be about your opinion of public figures, as you will learn after you have taken it – 'it ain't necessarily so!'

Personality Style Assessment

(A)   What cartoon character would Joan Collins be?

      SUPERMAN   BATMAN   CAPTAIN HOOK

(B)   What cartoon character would Margaret Thatcher be?

      SUPERMAN   BATMAN   CAPTAIN HOOK

(C)   What material would Joan Collins be?

      LEATHER   CHINA   PAPER

(D)   What car would Joan Collins be?

      PORSCHE   GOLF GTI

(E)   What Biblical character would you be?

      GOD   JESUS   ADAM

(F)   What material would Princess Diana be?

      LEATHER   CHINA   PAPER

(G)   What weapon would Princess Diana be?

      RIFLE   CANE

(H)   What car would Margaret Thatcher be?

      RACING CAR   GOLF GTI   MORRIS MINOR

(I)   What Biblical character would Princess Diana be?

      GOD   JESUS   ADAM

Results

The assessment you have done is about aspects of personality. We are not saying that your opinion of Joan Collins affects the way you lead people; however, research has shown that the character traits which make you answer these particular questions in a certain way would also have made you answer certain other questions in a particular way.

The benefit in using PSI here is that because you do not know what you are actually being asked about, it is very difficult to falsify one's answers, and present a chosen image to the world.

Now work out your score and see if you agree with the research findings.

Scoring
Follow the instructions below:

(a) Answers to this question show how much you want to be controlled by other people. Results are as follows:
Captain Hook: LOW
Batman   : MEDIUM
Superman   : HIGH

(b) Answers to this question and (c), (d) and (e) show how much you want to control and lead other people. Add up the numbers to get your final score.
Captain Hook: 1
Superman   : 2
Batman   : 3

(c) Leather   : 1
Paper   : 2
China   : 3

(d) Porsche   : 1
Golf GTi   : 3

(e) Adam   : 1
Jesus   : 2
God   : 3

		Total	
Adam	: 1	6 or below	LOW
Jesus	: 2	7 to 9	MEDIUM
God	: 3	10 to 12	HIGH

(f) Answers to this question and (g) show how sociable you would like to be. Results are as follows:

China : 1
Leather : 2
Paper : 3

Total
2 to 3   LOW

(g) Rifle : 1   4 to 5   MEDIUM
Cane : 3   6   HIGH

(h) Answers to this question show how sociable you are. Results are as follows:

Morris Minor : LOW
Golf GTi : MEDIUM
Racing Car : HIGH

(i) Answers to this question show how much affection you want. Results are as follows:

Adam : LOW
God : MEDIUM
Jesus : HIGH

Interpreting the Results
(OR HOW TO ADD SOME *S*LANDER TO THE *P*SYCHOLOGY)
Look at the results scored as a whole, you should be able to see a Personality Type at work.

Compare what people want to do, to what they actually achieve – imbalance means frustration or a fake front or over-demanding environment. This is particularly true of imbalance in the 'sociability' section.

Look at how people score on wishing to lead versus being led. People who score low on both are either loners, team players or dead.

People who are medium on both are balanced and comfortable with themselves. Imbalanced scores suggest frustration or being a fish out of water. Also look for correlations between areas. Someone who wants to lead but isn't sociable obviously lacks communication skills. Someone who doesn't like leading people but is very sociable may have their secret revealed in how much they need affection. It's worth noting that because people want to be led, it doesn't mean they act that way – it might be they long for someone strong enough to succeed in doing so!

In particular, look out for people who don't want affection, want to lead but aren't at all sociable and don't want to be – they could be dangerous psychopaths. (If this was your score, don't worry, we were only joking and are no longer living in England so it's fruitless looking for us.)

Personality types you should be able to spot are: born leaders, sheep, little boy/girl losts, life and soul of the party, losers, team players/committee members and attention seekers. If someone gets a perfect score, they are probably the inventors of this game – so congratulate them.

SECTION TWO: COMPATIBILITY

The following Psychology test uses the PSI technique to reveal a variety of different things about how you see yourself, and in particular about your relationship with your partner.

To do this test you and your partner will each need a piece of paper and a pen. Then, at the top of the page, copy out the diagram below:

	Question / Category	A/E If I was a ... which would I be?	B/F If I could be any of the ... which would I want to be?	C/G If my partner describes me as a ... I would be a:	D/H If my partner was a ... he/she would be a:
1	Animals	score	score	score	score
2	Parts of the body				
3	Birds				
4	Cars				
5	Places				

Please note, one of you should use the Headings A, B, C, D, at the top of each column, while the other marks them E, F, G and H.

Question A or E asks you to identify yourself as one of the animals/places listed.

Question B or F asks, if you could be any of the choices, what would you like to be most? In other words, you are describing your ideal self.

Question C or G asks what you think your partner would describe you as, if they had been asked the question.

Question D or H asks, if you had to describe your partner as one of the choices, which would it be?

Now simply take each column in turn and answer the questions shown for each of the five categories. For example, in the first column the five questions you must answer are:

If I were an Animal which would I be?

If I were a Part of the Body which would I be?

If I were a Bird which would I be?

If I were a Car which would I be?

If I were a Place which would I be?

In each case the choices available to you are listed on the following page. Pick whichever best sums up who you are if *you* were one item on that list.

This exercise must be repeated for each column, until the chart is filled in. You and your partner should do the exercise separately and without any form of conferring. To clarify what each column is asking you to consider, refer to the explanation above. To check the choices available to you in each category, use the list which follows.

Your answers should be honest; try to avoid going for insult or humour, just take the first natural choice that occurs to you. It is not necessary to know why you choose a particular answer; the best results come without thinking too long or too hard.

Category List

ANIMALS
Elephant   Snake

BIRDS
Sparrow   Swan

Horse   Lion   Chicken   Vulture
Mouse   Deer   Ostrich   Eagle
Pig

CARS   **PARTS OF THE BODY**
Mini   Reliant Robin   Feet   Hands
Rolls Royce Golf GTi   Head   Nipples
Sierra   Mercedes   Arms   Genitalia
             Transit Van

PLACES
Beirut   Barnsley
Paris   Costa del Sol
Rio   New York
Sydney   Monte Carlo
Kuala Lumpur   Brussels

When you have both filled in your sheets, look at the columns below, where each choice in each category is shown again with a score next to it. Look up the choice you have made and mark the score in the space provided on your sheets.

Do not get excited about how high or low the scores are, we are actually looking at how close the scores are together. The number given for your choice does not actually give it a value, this is done by your reaction to the explanation from the Lexicon.

ANIMALS   **BIRDS**
Elephant 9   Snake 1   Sparrow 7   Swan   9
Horse   9   Lion   8   Chicken 7   Vulture 0
Mouse   7   Deer   5   Ostrich 6   Eagle   9
Pig   10

CARS   **PARTS OF THE BODY**
Mini   7   Reliant Robin 1   Feet 6   Hands   7
Rolls Royce 9   Golf GTi   8   Head 9   Nipples 4
Sierra   9   Mercedes   9   Arms 7   Genitalia 5
                  Transit Van   5

PLACES
Beirut   10   Barnsley   0

Paris	6	Costa del Sol	3
Rio	6	New York	6
Sydney	6	Monte Carlo	5
Kuala Lumpur	4	Brussels	0

You now have two sheets which you have filled in with your choices and their scores. They should look something like this:

Your sheet

Question / Category	A If I was a ...	B If I could be any ...	C If my partner describes me as ...	D If my partner was a ...
1 Animals	Deer 8	Lion 8	Deer 8	Lion 8
2 Parts of the body	Head 9	Arm 5	Genitalia 7	Arm 5
3 Birds	Sparrow 7	Swan 9	Chicken 7	Eagle 9
4 Cars	Mini 7	Rolls Royce 9	Mini 7	Sierra 3
5 Places	Paris 6	New York 6	Paris 6	Barnsley 0

Your partner's sheet

Question / Category	E If I was a ...		F If I could be any ...		G If my partner describes me as ...		H If my partner was a ...	
1 Animals	Horse	9	Elephant	9	Horse	9	Mouse	7
2 Parts of the body	Head	5	Arm	9	Genitalia	7	Nipples	6
3 Birds	Chicken	7	Sparrow	9	Eagle	9	Swan	9
4 Cars	Mercedes	7	Rolls Royce	9	Mercedes	7	Mini	7
5 Places	New York	6	Rio	6	New York	6	Paris	6

Now all the work you've done becomes worthwhile. You are in a position to learn a lot about each other and your relationship as it currently stands. Go through the results section; each part will build up the picture.

(A) How I See Myself

First look up the various choices you have made in the Lexicon. This will give you a qualitative assessment of what kind of person you are, and what it means if you think of yourself in this light. The descriptions that appear consistently in different categories are strong personality traits, but you should expect to see some variation as most people have a variety of aspects to their personality.

(B)   How Accurate is My View of Myself?

This is where your partner's image of you comes in. The closer the two images are together, the more foundation there is for your view of yourself. First look up your partner's choices in the Lexicon: this will give you a feel for the differences that exist in your perceptions. To check how significant this difference of opinion actually is, deduct the scores in column H from those in column A. Your partner should do the same with columns D and E. When you do this you will obtain five numbers.

Category 1	H-A	=	x
Category 2	H-A	=	y
Category 3	H-A	=	z
Category 4	H-A	=	a
Category 5	H-A	=	b

Add them up, i.e. $x + y + z + a + b$ = total

When you do so, treat all the numbers as positive, i.e. $4 + (-2) = 6$

The total you get reflects the variance between how you think of yourself and how your partner thinks of you. The smaller the variation, the more foundation there is for your view.

If the total is:

5–7   You have good grounds for your opinions and view of yourself. You know who you are and so does your partner.

8–9   It is quite possible you tend to deceive yourself. Your partner certainly does not see you in quite the same light as you do yourself. If you feel your partner's opinion of you was higher than your own, you probably put yourself down (this is almost certainly the case if you also have a high total in assessment C, which follows). On the other hand, if their opinion seemed worse (and your score is low on the next assessment), they are probably right.

over 9   You have very different opinions. One of you is certainly wrong in their view of the other. The basis of your relationship is built on shaky ground which might not bear looking at. To check if you are at fault, do the next assessment; a low total suggests it's you.

(C) How Satisfied Am I With Myself?

Here you are comparing how you see yourself to your ideal self-image. The difference reflects how far you fall short of your 'goals', how satisfied you are with yourself and also sheds light on how accurate is your assessment of yourself.

Deduct your scores in column B from those in column A; your partner should do the same with columns F and E. Once again you will obtain five numbers.

Category 1	B-A	=	x
Category 2	B-A	=	y
Category 3	B-A	=	z
Category 4	B-A	=	a
Category 5	B-A	=	b

Add them up, i.e. $x + y + z + a + b =$ total

The total you get reflects the variance between how you actually think of yourself, and how you would like to think of yourself. The meaning of this is explained below.

Less than 7   This is very low. You are either extremely happy with yourself and see no area of possible improvement, or have an extremely high opinion of yourself. If your opinion is justified you will also have had a low variance in assessment B. You are fooling yourself, however, if your variance was high in B, for whereas you may think you are fulfilling your ambitions, the validity of your ability to assess this is in question! If your opinion of yourself was lower than your partner's, then the area to look at is why you are so convinced of your shortcomings. If your opinion of yourself was higher, you might seriously question why.

7–10   This is a healthy variance. You are aware of some room for improvement but basically are happy with yourself. If you scored well for accuracy in the last section, this is a particularly good result. If you didn't, you may be putting yourself down. If your partner valued you lower than your own assessment, you are possibly far too self-satisfied.

10–14   You either have a particular area of your personality that you would really like to change, or you are aware of many areas where you feel you don't quite do yourself justice. If you are right and others see you in the same light, that's fine; but you should learn to come to terms with who you are. If others see you closer to your ideal self, perhaps you should boost that self-image.

14+   You don't appear to be very pleased with yourself. Either you know what you are doing wrong in your own terms, but just cannot seem to change anything, or you seriously under-estimate yourself. Perhaps you are setting unrealistic targets. It may be very uncomfortable to have such a disparity between your current self-image and your ideal self.

(D)   How Well Do I Understand My Partner?

Here you are comparing your expectation of how your partner sees you (column C) with how they actually did (column H). The difference shows how well you know and understand each other, which is an important factor in long-term compatability. Your partner should use columns D and G.

Using the Lexicon, compare what you expected your partner's views to be with his/her actual opinions. The more inaccurate your assessment was, the less you understand your partner. Once again you can quantify the variance. This time, take the numbers in column H and deduct them from those in column C. Total up the numbers, ignoring their sign, i.e. $4 + (-5) = 9$. Your partner should use columns D and G in the same way.

Category 1   C-H   =   x
Category 2   C-H   =   y
Category 3   C-H   =   z
Category 4   C-H   =   a
Category 5   C-H   =   b

Add them up, i.e. $x + y + z + a + b =$ total

5–7   Very good, you know your partner well. If your score was also good on section B, you also know yourself, which is a great start for any relationship. As long as your partner scored nearly as high as you or equal to you, you are highly compatible and know where you are going.

7–9   There are some interesting differences here. You obviously don't know your partner quite as well as you thought. The areas you differ on will have come out using the Lexicon. They are unlikely to be major compatability problems, more probably areas that add a little fire to your relationship. If you have been scoring high variances in section B as well, you are a candidate for being a touch self-denigrating, believing your partner is blinded by love and does not see your faults. This may well be true, but either way you are doing OK in terms of compatibility. It's your self-image that needs looking at.

Over 9   You need to ask yourself some pretty serious questions. You have no idea of how your partner sees you. If they score as badly as you, then any degree of compatibility you feel is based on very loose grounds. Better start getting to know each other quickly or sort out why your opinions are so far apart. If your partner scored well and it's you who are misjudging him/her, look at your score in B. If that was high too, your ego is coming before your relationship. Be careful!

Overview

At the end of this assessment you should have a clear picture about the validity of your own opinions of yourself, and an accurate idea of how well you and your partner understand each other. These are both the vital ingredients of compatibility. Unless you like yourself you will find it hard to give to others, and unless you are able to see life from your partner's point of view you will not be able to deal effectively with the normal stresses and strains of a relationship.

It is important that you compare results of each section for both partners. There is a significant difference between both of you scoring inaccurately and one of you being the odd one out. If you both have inaccurate pictures of the other, you may well be compatible at the moment as your views effectively cancel each other out. The danger lies once this 'honeymoon' is over. Alternatively, if the fault is one-sided you had better address it now, as the harm to your compatibility has already started.

PSI: HOW IT ALL STARTED

PSI began as a bit of fun between friends, who invented their own form of slang when they discovered comparing people to an object painted a better picture than a thousand words. If one of them met a girl at a disco, they wouldn't ask, 'What colour hair did she have?' but, 'If she were a car, what make would she be?' If he said she was a Cadillac, they knew he was on to a good thing.

It turned out that this simple game worked so well that when shown to a team of psychologists they decided it could form the basis of a facinating new form of assessing aspects of personality.

It had taken Steve Knight and his friends over six years to develop the concept. Although they tried numerous toy companies, PSI only took off after a chance meeting with games whizz kid, Danny Kishon. He had set up a company called Paradigm devoted to publishing exciting new British games.

Within months PSI was not only set to be a huge success in Britain, it had been licensed to the rest of the world for an unprecedented seven-figure deal. This is the first time a British game has become the hottest property in America with over four million sets due to be sold.

So, what started as a form of slang has now become an international language and has turned Steve Knight into a games inventor, author and TV and radio writer. It has also introduced a new phrase into everyday vocabulary; when someone calls you a Surgical Stocking or a Bread and Butter Pudding with Cold Custard, remember they're only 'taking the PSI'.

PSI THE BOARD GAME IS AVAILABLE AT ALL GOOD STORES NOW, AT AROUND TWENTY POUNDS.

THE SEVEN DEADLY SINS

When you play PSI the board game, you begin the proceedings with an extremely telling personal decision.

Instead of picking something boring like a shoe or a ship or a coloured piece of plastic with which to play the game, you pick a deadly sin. And as if you didn't know, that means you have to choose between Pride, Gluttony, Avarice, Sloth, Anger, Envy or Lust.

The rules of PSI state that you must pick the deadly sin which you feel is most appropriate to your personality. And if that proves too embarrassing or revealing, one of your fellow players must pick your deadly sin for you.

Either way, the sin counter you end up with says a great deal about the person you *really* are. Just *how* much, is revealed in the final part of this book, the PSI players' guide to SIN.

Pride

If you pick Pride, you are a despicable coward. You have looked at all the other sins, decided that they are much too sordid, and gone for the one which at least has some respectable connotations.

Unfortunately for you, your choice has revealed more about you than you could imagine, because it is proof that you are actually hiding some sort of guilty secret. Pride is almost always a smokescreen for someone who is in reality racked with lust, driven by avarice or disabled by sloth. But you are so entrenched in your own deadly sin that you cannot bear to come clean and be honest about yourself. Such flagrant dishonesty ought to be penalised, but sadly the makers of the game are much too tolerant to give you your just desserts.

If Pride is picked for you, the message is almost as bad. To put it bluntly, for 'pride' read 'conceit'.

The person who picked Pride for you sees you as a vain, slightly pompous person. You are convinced that the world revolves around you and that absolutely everyone secretly admires you.

In fact, nothing could be further from the truth, and the most annoying thing of all about Pride people is that those around you are prepared to go to extraordinary lengths just to protect your eggshell ego.

Envy

If you pick Envy, you have a very specific problem: a sore point which involves not only you . . . but someone who is in the room, playing the game with you. (Pause for dramatic music.)

You have picked Envy for one simple reason. You are insanely, madly, rampantly jealous of one of your fellow players. It is possible to be this specific because Envy is not an emotion which you carry around with you as an intrinsic part of your personality. It is an ugly response to direct contact with a person who you feel is everything that you are not.

Take a look at the other players. One of them is almost certainly your Boss, your squash instructor, or your partner's secret lover. You hate this person so intensely that you have to see them just so that you can spend more time hating them. Remember, Envy is an ugly emotion, and the only cure is to get a new job, take a crash course in professional squash or get a new partner.

If Envy is picked for you, beware, you are involved in a 'Dallas'-style power struggle with the person who picked it. In an extremely complicated tangle of emotions, the person who thinks you are Envy secretly believes that you are a competitor who isn't up to the task. The only rational solution is pistols at dawn.

Avarice

If you pick Avarice, you are nursing secret ambitions. You want to be a world leader, a top financier, a pop star, a Captain of Industry, a Third World dictator, or even a Traffic Warden.

Your megalomania in your own fantasy world knows no bounds. Unfortunately, in the real world, you are one of life's no account nobodies. The person who chooses avarice is expressing an unfulfilled desire to control, acquire and dominate, a desire which, sadly, only ever finds expression in 'burning off' milk floats at the traffic lights.

If Avarice is picked for you, then all is not lost. The person who calls you Avarice sees you as someone who has managed to make a succes of their life, either financially or emotionally. However, since they see you as a competitor (see Envy), they are not prepared to give you a good old-fashioned slap on the back. Instead, they'd like to insert a knife into it.

Don't be too alarmed by the Avarice tag. See it as a kind of compliment, even if it is delivered through clenched teeth.

Gluttony

If you describe yourself as Gluttony, you're fat.

There it is, in black and white. You know it, the other players know it, everyone knows it. However every cloud has a silver lining, and the silvery bit for a Glutton is that at least you're fat and happy. You haven't, for example, sidestepped the issue by calling yourself Avarice and pretended that your hoglike habits are somehow related to your appetite for life. You eat too much, drink too much, do everything too much, but you love every minute of it.

(If you're genuinely *not* fat, you've picked Gluttony in order to hide something more sinister. Please pick again.)

If Gluttony is picked for you, you're fat.

There it is, in black and white. You know it, the other players know it, everyone knows it. However, this time, there's no silver lining. The person who picked Gluttony for you is acutely aware of your ample dimensions and your penchant for lard sandwiches, but is convinced that *you* are not aware of it.

You should therefore treat it as a not-so-gentle dig, and an attempt to make you change your ways. In almost every case, you'll find that the person who describes you as Gluttony is your partner.

Sloth

If you pick Sloth, you don't have to be told not to worry. For you, worrying is just too much effort. You are a drifter, a thinker, a do-as-you-please philosopher who never quite gets round to sorting out life's problems.

This is not to say that you are necessarily a lazy person. Indeed, you probably have an extremely alert and active mind. It's just that nothing that is on offer in your life excites you enough to make you spring into action, or even get out of your armchair.

There is very little wrong with this attitude, since while you're doing nothing, you can't be doing any harm.

If Sloth is picked for you, it's a different story. You really are a lazy person, someone who manages to surround themselves with things that need to be done, but lacks the will to do them. Sloth people are capable of half-mowing a lawn, of leaving the hall stairs painted half white and half maroon, and of owning a car for ten years without ever opening the bonnet.

Most worrying of all, if your partner called you Sloth, they are obviously suffering as a result of your lethargy, and unless you kick off your slippers and change your ways, they're going to leave you to go to seed like the couch potato you really are.

Anger

If you pick Anger, for goodness' sake remember your blood pressure before you read this character assassination, and please don't take it too seriously.

As an Anger person, you are the original beetroot-faced, complaining neighbour, the person at the back of the queue who insists that everyone get a move-on, the motorist who uses his horn instead of his head. You are convinced that everyone around you was put on this earth just to make your life difficult, and you're never afraid to let them know about it.

Be warned, Mr or Ms Anger, if you carry on like this, you will lose the few friends you have, and do your ticker untold damage in the process.

Take a tip from Sloth . . . just relax.

If Anger is picked for you, then you have every reason to feel rather pleased with yourself. To be seen as Anger actually denotes a great deal of respect. The person who picked it for you is impressed by your physical and emotional power, and is prepared to bow to your superior intellect.

However, involved in the Anger description there is an element of fear. You are seen as someone who should never be crossed, someone who demands the best and won't suffer fools at all. Perhaps you should take the trouble to smile occasionally, or at least grin. You never know, you might even enjoy it.

Lust

If you pick Lust, prepare to be unmasked, defrocked and debunked. For you are the sort of despicable character who has car stickers which say things like 'This car's rockin', don't come knockin!', or 'Windsurfers do it standing up', etc., etc.

Your tea mug probably says 'qualified sex instructor' on it, you wear your keys dangling from your belt, you have furry dice in your car.

Sadly for you and anyone foolish enough to take you as a partner, you are all mouth and tight denims. In reality, you see sex as something to be afraid of and you hide your fear in a flood of innuendo, nudges, winks and sexual boasts. When push comes to shove, you are in fact a bit of a flop, and you would have been far more accurate if you had picked Sloth.

If Lust is picked for you, then you are on the receiving end of what top doctors call 'emotion transference'. (We just made that bit up.)

To put it simply, the person who picked Lust for you actually fancies you like mad. They want you to believe that you are Lust because they can only think of you in sexual terms. It's what doctors call 'being in with a chance'.

Our advice to you is to put down the book, put down the game, and explore this fascinating psychological relationship a little more deeply.

india.